VENEZUELA

Jane Kohen Winter

MARSHALL CAVENDISH
New York • London • Sydney

Reference edition published 1991 by
Marshall Cavendish Corporation
2415 Jerusalem Avenue
P.O. Box 587
North Bellmore
New York 11710

© Times Editions Pte Ltd 1994, 1991

Originated and designed by
Times Books International, an imprint of
Times Editions Pte Ltd

Printed in Singapore

Library of Congress Cataloging-in-Publication Data:
Winter, Jane Kohen, 1959–
    Venezuela / Jane Kohen Winter.
      p. cm.—(Cultures Of The World)
    Includes bibliographical references and index.
    Summary: Introduces the geography, history,
    culture, and lifestyles of Venezuela.
    ISBN 1-85435-386-1
    1. Venezuela. [1. Venezuela.] I. Title. II. Series.
F2308.5.W56 1991
987—dc20   90–22470
               CIP
               AC

Cultures of the World

Editorial Director	Shirley Hew
Managing Editor	Shova Loh
Editors	Roseline Lum
	Michael Spilling
	Siow Peng Han
	Leonard Lau
	MaryLee Knowlton
	Azra Moiz
	Mario Sismondo
	Kamariah Abdul Rahim
	June Khoo Ai Lin
	Kieran Falconer
	Sue Sismondo
Picture Editors	Jane Duff
	Mee-Yee Lee
Production	Edmund Lam
Design	Tuck Loong
	Felicia Wong
	Lee Woon Hong
	Dani Phoa
	Ong Su Ping
	Katherine Tan
Illustrators	Thomas Koh
	Anwar bin Abdul Rahim
MCC Editorial Director	Evelyn M. Fazio
MCC Production Manager	Ruth Toda

INTRODUCTION

VENEZUELA is truly a land of superlatives. It is the wealthiest nation in Latin America, thanks to its petroleum reserves. It contains some of the world's oldest and most mysterious geologic formations, the world's highest waterfall, and some of its rarest and most unusual flowers, fish, birds, and animals.

Venezuelans can also be described in terms of superlatives. The people of Venezuela's capital city of Caracas (called *caraqueños*) are some of the most sophisticated in Latin America, and the cowboys of the grasslands are some of the hardest-working. Each year, they battle both the floods of the wet season and the drought of the dry season in an attempt to feed their cattle. Simón Bolívar, one of South America's most revered heroes and the father of independence for several South American nations, was born in Caracas.

In this book, one of the series *Cultures of the World*, we will explore the land, people, and lifestyle of a remarkable South American country.

CONTENTS

Venezuelan children of the Andes with their mules, near Pico Bolívar, the country's tallest peak.

CONTENTS

A Venezuelan girl of African origin.

GEOGRAPHY

VENEZUELA, the seventh largest country in South America, lies at the north of the continent. With an area of more than 352,000 square miles, Venezuela is about the size of the states of Texas and Oklahoma combined, four times the size of Great Britain, 28 times that of Holland, but only one-tenth the size of Brazil. Its coastline is 2,000 miles long and abuts both the Caribbean Sea and the Atlantic Ocean. Half of Venezuela is covered by forests and beaches; mountains, plains, deserts, and grasslands make up the other half.

THE VENEZUELAN HIGHLANDS

Venezuela can be divided into four distinct geographic regions. The first area, the Venezuelan Highlands, lies in the west and along the coast, and includes the Andean mountain range within the Venezuelan border. Though representing only 12% of Venezuela's land area, it contains 66% of its population and most of its major cities. Caracas, the capital city of Venezuela and one of the wealthiest and most modern capitals in the world, lies in this region.

Opposite: **The Caribbean coast in north Venezuela.**

Below: **Pico Bolívar, the tallest peak in Venezuela, shortly before sunset, seen from another mountain.**

Caracas (four million inhabitants) has a most pleasant climate; it has been called "Los Angeles without the smog." With a new French-designed subway system, a skyline of high-rise office buildings, and apartment houses, Caracas is one of the most sophisticated cities in Latin America and the world. Unfortunately, the capital is as poor as it is wealthy; thousands of inhabitants live in *ranchos* ("RAHN-chohs," makeshift shacks) on the fringes of the city.

"…a wide and stretching land, all horizons like hope, all roads like the will."

—*Rómulo Gallegos, describing the* llanos *in his novel,* Doña Bárbara

The *llanos* are Venezuela's main grazing land. A single spark in the scorching heat of the dry season can cause extensive damage.

8

THE MARACAIBO LOWLANDS

The second major geographical region of Venezuela, the Maracaibo Lowlands, lies in the northwest of the country. This area contains Lake Maracaibo, the largest lake in South America. This shallow freshwater lake is 75 miles long and 100 miles wide. At the northern tip, where the lake opens into the Caribbean Sea, lies the port of Maracaibo. In the early part of the 20th century, the most important oil wells in Venezuela were discovered there. Now, the lake is dotted with thousands of oil derricks that extract millions of barrels of oil each year. With a population of more than one million, the city of Maracaibo is the second largest city in Venezuela. It is reached via the five-mile-long General Raphael Urdaneta Bridge, the longest prestressed concrete bridge in the world.

THE PLAINS

The third region in Venezuela is the plains, or *llanos* ("YAH-noss"), located in the central part of the country. The *llanos* cover nearly one-third of Venezuela, yet hold only 9% of the population. This low population density is due to the extremely harsh landscape and climate. The land is flat and almost treeless, and the climate ranges from scorchingly hot and dry to penetratingly damp and muggy, depending on the season. Five million heads of cattle live in the *llanos*. The herds are driven by Venezuelan cowboys, or *llaneros* ("yah-NAIR-rohs"), to wetter areas during the dry season and to drier areas during the wet season.

Los Nevados is one of the highest villages in Venezuela. The vegetation is far more interesting than that found on the *llanos* (*see opposite*), and conditions are more suitable for settlers.

THE GUIANA HIGHLANDS

In the south and east of Venezuela lie the Guiana Highlands, which constitute the fourth geographic region of the country. They take up almost half the nation's land, yet are nearly uninhabited. The Guiana Highlands are covered with ancient, vast sandstone rock formations called *tepuis* ("tair-POO-ees"), or tablelands, which can reach as high as 6,000 feet. Their bases are carved by erosion into different types of relief. Many *tepuis* are virtually unscalable, leaving much of the Guiana Highlands unexplored, even today.

A cloud-topped *tepui*

The Guiana Highlands also contain the world's highest waterfall, Angel Falls, first spotted by pilot James Angel in 1935 while he was searching for gold. At 3,212 feet, the falls are more than 15 times taller than Niagara Falls, or twice the height of New York's Empire State Building. Strangely enough, Angel Falls does not flow over a cliff. The water actually accumulates underground and erupts through cracks in the mountain.

The largest city in the Guiana Highlands, Guayana (500,000 inhabitants), is the fifth largest city in Venezuela and a hub of heavy industry.

THE ISLANDS

Venezuela also possesses 72 islands in the Caribbean Sea. The most popular of these, Margarita Island, known for its beaches and colonial architecture, is a favorite resort for Venezuelans and tourists.

THE LOST WORLD OF ARTHUR CONAN DOYLE

Sir Arthur Conan Doyle, creator of the Sherlock Holmes detective stories, wrote a fantasy-adventure tale about the Guiana Highlands. *The Lost World*, originally published in 1912, is an account of an expedition by four English adventurers to a remote region in Venezuela. This region, cut off from the outside world, still contained prehistoric creatures such as 20-foot pterodactyls, enormous three-toed, black-skinned dinosaurs, and apemen.

"South America is a place I love. …It's the grandest, richest, most wonderful bit of earth upon this planet. …Why shouldn't somethin' new and wonderful lie in such a country? And why shouldn't we be the men to find out?" asks one of the characters in *The Lost World*.

Even today, scientists and adventurers consider exploring the *tepuis* of the Guiana Highlands an enormous challenge. An explorer on Mt. Roraima, the rock formation described in *The Lost World* that actually dates back 1.8 billion years, reported that he was awakened by a frightening, inexplicable scream as he camped on the rock. A similar shriek was vividly recounted by the book's narrator and later attributed to a dinosaur.

The picture-pretty Guiana Highlands challenge adventurous climbers.

Above right: **Tropical rain forest of the Orinoco region.**

Opposite: **Both photographs show the same area of the *llanos*: one in the wet season and one in the dry season.**

THE GREAT ORINOCO RIVER

The Orinoco River, with its 436 tributaries, is the third longest river in South America and the eighth longest in the world. It flows 1,370 miles from its source in the Guiana Highlands close to Brazil, diverges into 100 separate channels, and rushes with such great force into the Atlantic Ocean that there is fresh water for miles out to sea.

The Orinoco River and the great Amazon River actually connect at one point through a waterway called the Casiquiare Canal. It is said that together they form the greatest river system in the world. They carry more water and drain a larger area than both the Missouri-Mississippi system and the Nile. In fact, more than a third of South America—approximately 2.5 million square miles—is dominated by the Orinoco-Amazon system. The Orinoco also provides important communication links with the interior of Venezuela and hydroelectric power for a good part of the country.

CLIMATE

Although all of Venezuela lies within the tropical zone, temperatures vary among the regions, depending on elevation and prevailing winds. Basically, the country has three temperature zones: the "hot land" (Maracaibo, for example), where it is quite humid and average daily temperatures exceed 75°F but rarely top 95°F; the "temperate land" (Caracas, for example), where average daily temperatures range from 50°F to 80°F; and the "cold land" (in the mountainous areas of the country), where temperatures are below 65°F during the day and drop to freezing point at night. Only on the highest Andean peaks can you find snow all year round.

During the wet season—May to October—the *llanos* and forest areas are swampy and green. During the dry season, however, those same areas become parched and brown. Rainfall averages less than 20 inches on the mountainous coast. In the southern part of the Maracaibo Lowlands and in the Orinoco River delta, the rainfall can go up to 80 inches annually. The high plateaus of the Guiana Highlands receive only moderate rainfall. Caracas gets about 32 inches a year (the same amount as Chicago).

Venezuela's national tree, the *aranguery* ("ah-rahn-goo-eh-REE"), grows almost everywhere in the country. When it blooms, it erupts in vibrant yellow flowers that stand out against the green of the rest of the landscape.

FLORA

Venezuela has more species of plants than the United States and Canada combined. In the mountains, below 3,000 feet, tropical forests with dense shrubbery are most common. Between 3,000 and 6,000 feet, there is scrubby woodland and dense forest filled with exotic orchids. The Venezuelan national flower, an orchid with elegant deep pink petals, is found at this altitude.

Above 6,000 feet, vegetation is sparse. Grasses and herbaceous plants are most common. In the alpine regions, from 10,000 to 15,000 feet, there is little plant life. High pastures are most common here, but the yellow flowering *frailejón* ("fray-lay-KHON") tree helps break up the landscape. Its leaves, resembling rabbits' ears, have been used as mattress stuffing.

In the Maracaibo region, the high humidity and heavy rainfall have resulted in lush tropical forests. Near the Caribbean Sea, however, the air is drier, and desert plants are more common.

The *llanos* are Venezuela's natural pasture, thanks to the light soils and alternating wet and dry seasons. To the east, in the Orinoco River delta, the land is swampy and full of mangrove thickets.

Most of the Guiana Highlands is covered with rough natural grass and semideciduous tropical forest tangled with vines and parasitic growth. Rare plant varieties are found on the *tepuis* of the Roraima group. Fifteen years ago, an orchid specialist discovered 61 species—some never seen before by botanists—in a five-acre area of an almost soilless *tepui*.

FAUNA

In the Venezuelan Highlands, big cats such as jaguars, ocelots, and pumas are evident, as well as varieties of monkeys, bears, deer, wild pigs, otters, sloths, anteaters, foxes, opossums, armadillos, and rodents.

The lowlands of the *llanos* compare with the African continent in variety and quantity of animal species, including big game. Many species that are now threatened elsewhere have survived here because of the low human population.

Besides the five million cattle that roam the *llanos*, this central region of Venezuela has some of the world's most unusual species.

The capybara, which lives in the swampy areas, has the distinction of being the world's largest rodent. It can weigh up to 100 pounds, and looks more like a friendly beaver or otter than a giant rat. The capybara has partially webbed toes, no tail, and a cleft palate. It eats only plants and communicates by making a low grunting noise.

The Orinoco River contains a great variety of fish, including a species of catfish that can weigh up to 300 pounds. Rare river mammals such as the dolphin and the sea cow or manatee are also found in the fresh waters of the Orinoco.

The cycnoches chlorochilon *can carry 3.7 million seeds in a single pod. This is to guarantee propagation because many of the seeds will die before they germinate.*

The Orinoco dolphin has small eyes, pink skin, a long beak, and a humped back; it is rather unattractive as dolphins go (*see the dolphins at left*). Unlike other freshwater varieties, the Orinoco dolphin lives in schools of 12–20 and shows signs of group loyalty. Another smaller species of freshwater dolphin, which only reaches five to six feet in length, is considered sacred by some local Indians. This variety (*below left*) has the "smiling" face commonly associated with the ocean swimming bottle-nosed dolphin.

The Orinoco crocodile, one of the 12 most-endangered species in the world, also makes its home in the *llanos*. Between 1920 and 1940, almost two million Orinoco crocodiles were killed for their magnificent hides. Some of the male crocs were said to weigh up to a ton. German naturalist Alexander von Humboldt, who explored the Orinoco early in the 1800s, reported seeing crocodiles that measured as long as 24 feet. Now, despite the collapse of the hide industry and serious conservation attempts on all sides, only 2,000–5,000 of these reptiles exist in both Venezuela and Colombia.

Each new exploration into the Guiana Highlands yields new animal species that were never documented before. The harsh environment has kept the area clear of visitors and has forced many plants and animals to develop interesting survival tactics. A recent expedition uncovered a species of toad with feet specially adapted for climbing rocky cliffs and a catfish with a full-fledged beard (not just whiskers) used to attract mates.

The giant otter of the Orinoco River area

In the famous Guácharo Cave in northeast Venezuela lives the oilbird, or *guácharo* ("goo-AH-chah-roh"), which has been an object of curiosity since 1799 when Humboldt told the scientific world of its existence. Ten thousand oilbirds live in the Guácharo Cave, within the boundaries of a 34,000-acre park reserve.

The oilbird is reddish-brown, with a wing span of more than three feet. The bird is nocturnal, just like a bat. During the day, it sleeps crowded together with other birds in the black caves. If awakened, it lets out a disturbing cry. At dusk, it flies out to find food, using echolocation. The only food that seems to interest the oilbird is the oily nut of the palm. The oilbird got its name in the early 1800s when it was hunted by Indians and missionaries for its fat, which was made into lamp oil. Today, it is illegal to kill an oilbird.

COLON EN EL GOLFO TRISTE

HISTORY

THE SEARCH FOR GOLD shaped Venezuela's early history—even though gold is not found there in great quantity.

According to myth, a "gilded man," or "El Dorado," was said to have made his kingdom in northern South America. This Indian chief was supposed to have been so wealthy that he went about dusted in gold. Each night he washed it off, only to reapply it the next morning.

With dreams of possessing the kingdom of El Dorado, European explorers traveled to present-day Venezuela in the last years of the 15th century. When Christopher Columbus reached the coast in the 1490s, he wrote to his king and queen to claim the land for Spain, and to tell of the Indians he had seen with pearls around their necks and arms.

Had they been able to travel to the 20th century, Columbus (*opposite*), Vespucci, and Ojeda would have recognized these Indian huts on stilts. Those above, however, are not on Lake Maracaibo, but are found in the Orinoco River delta.

In 1499, Spanish explorer Alfonso de Ojeda made a memorable expedition to the northern part of Venezuela. Seeing the Indian huts built on stilts in Lake Maracaibo, Ojeda and his mapmaker, Amerigo Vespucci (for whom America is named), were reminded of the canals of Venice, so they named the country "Little Venice," or Venezuela.

EARLIEST INHABITANTS

Like the rest of the Americas, Venezuela was originally inhabited by Indians, who, during the Ice Age, had made their way to South America from Asia across the Bering Strait. South America was populated between 10,000 and 20,000 B.C. by primitive hunters who fed on mastodons and giant sloths. By 1000 B.C. these hunters, the peaceful Arawak tribe, had become farmers. They were driven from the land by the warlike Caribs.

19

When Columbus first saw the Indians of Venezuela in October 1492, he described them as being "of tanned color…neither black nor white." They had black hair, "not kinky but straight and coarse like horsehair," broad foreheads, handsome eyes, and straight legs; "…no belly, but very well built," he wrote.

The Venezuelan Indians were accomplished farmers, great artisans, and rich in religious ritual, but they were not as highly organized as the Aztecs, Incas, or Mayas. Although they fought the Spanish conquistadors with great spirit, they were overcome.

SPANISH CONQUEST

In 1509, the first European settlement in all of South America was founded on the Venezuelan island of Cubagua. The settlers had come in search of pearls, but by 1550 the pearl beds were dry and the island was abandoned. In about 1520, the first permanent Spanish settlement was founded at Cumaná, on the northeast coast of Venezuela.

The town of Coro, founded in 1527, is significant in Venezuela's history. In order to pay his debts, Charles I of Spain mortgaged the town to the German banking house of Wesler. In search of El Dorado, the Weslers made expeditions into the Venezuelan interior, looting the country and killing many of the natives, but not finding any gold. In 1546, Spain terminated its agreement with the Germans and, giving up the search for gold, opted to develop Venezuela agriculturally.

By the end of the 16th century, 20 towns had been established. Many of the Indians were forced to become slaves on the sugar and coffee *haciendas* ("ah-sih-EHN-dahs," plantations) of the Spanish settlers. Millions of slaves died, and the landowners had to import African slaves from the Caribbean islands to work the fields. Although South America had nearly

50 million native Indians in the 15th century, by the end of the Conquest, only two million survived. Most of the remaining Indians, who lived in the *llanos* and Maracaibo regions, were colonized by the Dominican, Jesuit, Franciscan, and Augustinian missionaries from Spain who, by the early 1700s, had spread Christianity to remote parts of the country.

The male Spanish settlers, called *peninsulars* ("pay-nihn-SOO-lars"), held powerful positions and eventually intermarried with the native population, producing *mestizos* ("mehs-TEE-sohs"). *Criollos* ("kree-OH-lohs," Creoles), or people of Spanish heritage born in Venezuela, held prominent positions at the local level and resented the dominant class of *peninsulars*. The *criollos* also intermarried. The people of African origin who were brought over as slaves were considered the lowest class.

Left and opposite: **Evidence exists of the Spanish Conquest—in the forts and the religious institutions. Opposite is the Castillo or Fort of San Antonio de la Eminencia (1660), built to protect the coastal city of Cumaná from pirates. At left is La Casa Fuerte (originally the Convent of San Francisco) in Barcelona, Venezuela.**

"I desire more than anybody else to see the formation in America of the greatest nation in the world, not so much for its size and wealth, as for its freedom and glory."

—Simón Bolívar, in a letter from Jamaica, September 1815

THE INDEPENDENCE MOVEMENT

Like the U.S. Independence movement, the Venezuelan movement had its roots in the desire of Venezuelans to trade freely with other nations.

In 1728, the Real Compañia Guipuzcoana de Caracas was established, giving the Basques from Spain exclusive rights to import goods into Venezuela. In 1785, however, because of local jealousy and opposition to the monopoly of foreign trade by the Europeans, the company was dismantled and free trade was granted, but only within the Spanish Empire.

In 1797, Britain occupied the island of Trinidad for the purpose of selling goods illegally to Venezuela. To foil British attempts, Spain decided to allow free trade between all nations. However, in 1802, the Spaniards changed their minds and decided once again to limit free trade. This angered many Venezuelans who, led by Francisco de Miranda, a *caraqueño* ("kah-rah-KAIR-nyoh," native of Caracas), revolted, beginning the Independence movement.

This initial foray into self-rule was not successful, however, and

Miranda was exiled. In 1810, he returned and on July 5, 1811, he was proclaimed dictator of Venezuela, which now had a population of about 700,000, 60% of African heritage. By 1812, Miranda was captured by the forces still in favor of Spanish rule.

Simón Bolívar, also a *caraqueño* and Miranda's former aide, invaded Venezuela in 1813, reestablished the republic (with himself as dictator), and was given the title of Liberator. Unfortunately, the republic was destroyed again in 1814 by a group of cowboys, or *llaneros* from the plains who still had royalist leanings. Bolívar was forced into exile, but he returned in 1817 to establish the third republic.

In 1819, Bolívar devised a grand scheme to bring Venezuela, what is now Colombia, and Ecuador together into one independent state called Gran Colombia. It was not until 1821, however, that he succeeded in accomplishing his scheme by defeating the Spanish in the Battle of Carabobo. In 1830, Venezuela seceded from Gran Colombia and became truly independent. José Antonio Páez, who had expelled the last Spanish garrison in 1823, was named president.

LA GRAN COLOMBIA

SIMÓN BOLÍVAR, THE LIBERATOR

Simón Bolívar is Venezuela's most revered citizen. Born in Caracas to wealthy *criollo* parents in 1783, Bolívar traveled to Europe in 1799 and 1803. In France, he was influenced by the revolutionary spirit of the Parisians, who inspired his dream of independence for Venezuela.

Bolívar was a thin, small man, with a lean face and vibrant black eyes. A good horseman and swimmer, he is said to have had an amazing amount of energy. His soldiers were devoted to him, and the British Romantic poet, Lord Byron, was so enamored of him that he named his boat *Bolivar* and actually made plans to move to Venezuela with his daughter.

Bolívar was a brilliant orator and his speeches are still read and respected today. In 1812, when Caracas was destroyed by an earthquake, he said, "If Nature opposes our designs, we shall fight against her and make her obey." Bolívar died in 1830 at age 47.

THE TURBULENT ROAD TO DEMOCRACY

The 19th century was a time of political instability and dictatorial rule for Venezuela. The early 20th century was dominated by a fierce dictator named General Juan Vicente Gómez who, with the army and police under his control, ruled from 1908 to 1935 by repression and terror. Venezuelans danced in the streets when they heard of his death. Petroleum, which made Venezuela the real El Dorado, was discovered in 1914 during Gómez's rule.

Although between 1936 and 1948 Venezuela was ruled democratically (the country's most famous novelist, Rómulo Gallegos, was elected president during this time), the mid-20th century was also a time of political unrest. From 1950 to 1958, Venezuela was under the control of

General Marcos Pérez Jiménez, another dictator. His tenure was marked by corruption and brutal suppression of the opposition. He is remembered, however, for building roads and housing projects in Caracas.

It was not until 1958 that Rómulo Betancourt and his democratic party (Acción Democrática, or AD) brought true and lasting democracy to Venezuela. Betancourt is famous for his philosophy of "sowing the oil," or using the profits from petroleum revenues to benefit the people of Venezuela. During his term, he tackled problems of illiteracy, poor living conditions and educational facilities, and the high infant mortality rate.

Since the 1960s, the AD party and the other strong political party, the Social Christian Party (COPEI), have been in power. They have similar aims: to improve the lives of the poor and to modernize industry and agriculture.

AD candidate Carlos Andrés Pérez was elected president in 1974 and again in 1989, after the requisite 10-year waiting period. During his first term, Pérez nationalized the petroleum industry and launched ambitious programs in education and agriculture. In foreign relations, Venezuela, through Pérez, has become an important advocate of human rights and economic independence.

In the 1980s, Venezuela experienced a severe economic blow due to the oil gluts of 1979–80 and 1986.

In 1992, Pérez survived two coup attempts led by the military. In May 1993, however, he was suspended as president when the Senate authorized the Supreme Court to try him on charges of misappropriating $17 million in government funds. Later, in August, the Congress made permanent the Senate's suspension, meaning that Pérez could not return as president of Venezuela even if he were acquitted of the corruption charges.

Elections for a new president took place in December 1993.

"I will never allow my hands to be idle or my soul to rest until I have broken the shackles which chain us to Spain."

—*Simón Bolívar, as a student in Europe*

GOVERNMENT

THE REPUBLIC OF VENEZUELA is one of Latin America's oldest functioning democracies. It is made up of 20 states, two federal territories (Amazonas and Delta Amacuro), 72 islands, and the Federal District of Caracas. In 1985, the states were subdivided into 156 districts and 613 municipalities.

Like the U.S. system, the Venezuelan government can be divided into three distinct groups: the executive, legislative, and judicial branches.

THE EXECUTIVE BRANCH

The chief executive of Venezuela, the president of the republic, is elected by the people for a five-year term and cannot be elected for consecutive terms. The outgoing president of Venezuela, Carlos Andrés Pérez, was president before, from 1974 to 1979, but could not run again until 1989, 10 years after his first term was completed.

Ex-presidents of the country are members of the Senate for life. Presidents must be native-born Venezuelans and at least 30 years old. Their duties include:

- selecting and removing the 24 cabinet ministers and all other administrative officers and employees of the national government;
- commanding the armed forces;
- directing foreign affairs;
- making and ratifying international treaties, conventions, and agreements;
- declaring a state of emergency, if necessary;
- ordering the suspension of constitutional guarantees, if necessary; and
- introducing bills and defending them before Congress.

Opposite: **The Capitol, the government building in Caracas.**

Below: **The Elliptic Salon of the Federal Palace in Caracas, on the ceiling of which is painted the Battle of Carabobo, scene of Simón Bolívar's triumph.**

In Venezuela, the president has no deputy or vice-president. In the event of the president's death, disability, or resignation, the Congress must select a new president by secret ballot within 30 days.

The president has the right to veto any decisions taken by the Congress, and the latter needs a two-thirds majority to override a presidential veto.

Voting is compulsory. All Venezuelan citizens over the age of 18 must vote in presidential elections, according to Venezuelan law. Only prisoners and members of the armed forces are exempt. Voter turnout at every election is more than 80%.

In Trujillo, a government employee gives a talk on "intelligence development," as part of the government's plan to educate Venezuelans in the more remote regions.

THE LEGISLATIVE BRANCH

The Venezuelan Congress is made up of a Senate and a Chamber of Deputies. Each state may elect two senators, but the number of deputies elected is in accordance with population figures. (This is similar to the system used in the U.S. Congress, where there are two senators from each of the 50 states, but varying numbers of representatives per state in the House of Representatives.)

Senators and deputies are also elected for five-year terms. Senators must be at least 30 years old, while deputies need only be over 21. To be eligible for election to the Senate or the Chamber of Deputies, candidates must be native-born.

THE JUDICIAL BRANCH

Ultimate judicial power is held by the Supreme Court of Justice. Supreme Court judges are elected by Congress for nine-year terms. A third of the judges are newly elected every three years. Decisions made by the Supreme Court cannot be appealed, as it is the highest court in the land. It can declare a law or an act of the president unconstitutional, and it can determine whether or not the president and members of Congress can be put on trial.

Venezuelan soldiers on parade in Caracas

Each state has its own supreme court as well as lower courts. The jury system is not practiced in Venezuela, and the maximum prison sentence is 30 years.

STATES, DISTRICTS, AND MUNICIPALITIES

Individual states in Venezuela have limited powers, despite the fact that they elect their own legislatures. Each state operates on funds allocated by the national government. The Congress writes the laws and makes decisions regarding education, health, and agricultural issues. Until recently, the president even appointed state governors; now they are elected by their constituents.

The states are subdivided into districts and municipalities. Local governments are run by city councils made up of five to 22 members, depending on the size of the population. Council members are elected by the people.

THE VENEZUELAN CONSTITUTION

The first Venezuelan constitution was adopted on December 21, 1811, almost six months after independence from Spain was declared. The original document was influenced by the American and French constitutions, but was not based on them.

In Maracaibo, a mother makes her baby exercise, as she has been taught to do by a government social worker.

Since 1811, the constitution has been rewritten 24 times, usually in times of political upheaval. The 22nd constitution, adopted in 1945, gave women the right to vote, and the 23rd version (1947) ensured the separation of church and state and increased the authority of the federal government. The 24th constitution (1953) changed the country's official name to the Republic of Venezuela. Currently, the republic is governed by the document adopted in January 1961.

Like the U.S. Constitution, the Venezuelan constitution advocates personal liberties and human equality. The introduction states that all Venezuelans have the right to social and legal equality, "without discrimination due to race, sex, creed, or social conditions." One of the constitution's aims, it states, is to support democracy as the sole means of ensuring the rights and dignity of citizens. The constitution also refers to Simón Bolívar as the Liberator of Venezuela.

Two articles of the constitution proclaim the right to freedom of religion and expression, and another allows for freedom of peaceful assembly.

The constitution requires the State to provide an education for all citizens as well as to oversee the maintenance of public health. The government promises to try to improve the living conditions of the rural population and to protect the Indian communities and help them integrate into the life of the nation.

In return, the constitution declares that the State expects all Venezuelans to "honor and defend their country and to safeguard and protect the interests of the Nation." Military service is compulsory, as is education, and "labor is a duty of every person fit to perform it."

THE GOVERNMENT'S GOALS

The Venezuelan government's current goals are to:

- preserve and protect free and democratic institutions, and maintain public order;
- strengthen and modernize the armed forces;
- eliminate the conditions in society that foster crime;
- upgrade law enforcement;
- refinance the debt owed to other nations without affecting living standards of Venezuelan citizens;
- improve the country's physical infrastructure to encourage agricultural development; and
- reorient the industries to produce essential goods to meet basic needs, generate jobs, and fight inflation.

Carlos Andrés Pérez, president of Venezuela from 1974 to 1979, was elected once again in 1989. He resigned in 1993 following impeachment charges brought against him by the Supreme Court.

ECONOMY

IN THE LATE 1970s, during President Carlos Andrés Pérez's first term, Venezuela was at the height of economic prosperity: oil revenue was pouring in; new petrochemical, steel, and hydroelectric plants were being built on a large scale; ships from foreign countries were lined up at Venezuelan ports ready to deliver luxury goods to *caraqueños*; and the wealthiest Venezuelans were traveling abroad on shopping sprees or to study at foreign universities.

By the early 1980s, the economic story was entirely different: the worldwide oil glut had decreased Venezuela's oil revenue, crippling the nation's ability to repay its foreign debt; prices increased dramatically; and people's salaries were frozen or jobs lost. Even food staples like salt, rice, and sugar were difficult to get.

The Venezuelan economy has been so dominated by petroleum since the discovery of oil in 1914—oil revenue formerly made up more than two-thirds of the government's income and more than 90% of Venezuela's exports—that when oil revenues fall, so does the entire financial structure of the country. Presently, although the economy has recovered to some extent, the country has had to refocus, to try to develop other industries that do not rely so heavily on petroleum.

The current government has four goals toward economic recovery: (1) cut down on the number of government workers by letting private companies take over public services; (2) remove laws that obstruct efficiency and competition; (3) encourage foreign companies to invest in Venezuela; and (4) shift the economy away from oil and into new export industries like steel, gold, cocoa, coffee, tropical fruits, and petrochemicals. The government also wants to lure tourists to the fine beaches of Margarita Island and to the sophisticated shopping malls and fine restaurants of Caracas.

Opposite: **Oil rigs on Lake Maracaibo pumping "black gold."**

The Ciudad Guayana Industrial Complex produces iron ore, paper, and aluminum.

FACTS AND FIGURES

Currently, earnings from petrochemicals, oil refining, manufacturing, construction, and trade make up 60% of Venezuela's Gross Domestic Product (GDP). Agricultural products—which make up 5.5% of the GDP—include rice, coffee, corn, sugar, bananas, dairy products, meat, and poultry.

In 1992, Venezuela's principal exports included petroleum and its derivatives, metals, chemicals, cars, and car parts worth almost $13 billion. In the same year, the majority of imports included transport equipment, machinery, chemicals, and metals totaling nearly $9 billion.

Venezuela's main trading partners are the United States, Germany, Japan, Brazil, Italy, and the Netherlands.

PETROLEUM AND MINING

Before the discovery of petroleum beneath the surface of Lake Maracaibo, Venezuela was a relatively poor country of farmers. Many necessary consumer goods had to be imported from overseas. Once oil was found, however, rapid changes took place, bringing immense wealth to the country, but not to most of its people. Foreign oil companies were brought in to remove and process the oil, and the corrupt Venezuelan dictators in power at the time made handsome profits.

When Rómulo Betancourt took control of the government in 1959, he used the profits from the oil industry to fund much-needed social programs. He directed the foreign oil companies to train Venezuelans and demanded that the foreigners pay a higher percentage of their profits to the Venezuelan government. Before the 1960s, most of the oil in Venezuela was refined outside the country and natural gas was wasted. Now, Venezuela has its own refineries and gas is saved for fuel and other uses.

About 75% of the nation's oil comes from the Lake Maracaibo region. Other reserves are in the northern *llanos*, the Apure-Barinas river basin in the west, and in the east. As these reserves are quite limited, exploration has been made both into the Orinoco River delta and offshore.

After petroleum, iron ore is the country's most important natural resource. Much of it is used domestically in the steel industry, as are nickel, zinc, and coal. Bauxite, discovered in the 1970s, is used in the aluminum industry.

"Our country is rich but our people are poor."

—*ex-President Carlos Andrés Pérez*

A sponge-iron mill in Orinoco

The Guri Dam at the
Caroní River

MANUFACTURING AND POWER

In an attempt at diversification, Venezuela has recently begun the exportation of aluminum products, manufactured in the city of Ciudad Guayana.

Most of the manufacturing of consumer goods—food, tobacco, textiles, clothing, wood, paper, and plastic items—takes place in the northern cities. In Caracas, factories produce glass, chemicals, pharmaceuticals, processed food, and leather goods, among other products.

Venezuela has huge electric power dams on the Caroní River, and Venezuelans enjoy one of the best electrical energy services in Latin America. Power outages or electrical surges are seen much less frequently in Venezuela than in other nearby countries.

AGRICULTURE

During the oil boom of the 1970s, Venezuela's agricultural potential was not exploited. Eggs came from Miami, Florida, meat from Argentina, and vegetables from Chile. While in the 1930s agriculture provided 70% of the GDP, by 1992 it provided only 5.5%, and 74% of the country's food was imported.

With the fall of oil prices and the economic crisis that ensued came plans to develop Venezuela's agriculture. Unfortunately, by 1988, only about 13% of the population still worked in agriculture. Many people have moved to urban areas to pursue jobs away from the soil.

The government is now encouraging people to become farmers by providing them with credit, technical assistance, and machinery, but many young people prefer to stay in the cities. Some progress has been made on the *llanos* in the cattle-breeding areas, and in the cultivation of cocoa, coffee, and tropical fruits elsewhere.

With only about 2% of the country's arable land being used and many unemployed urban dwellers, there is obviously much room for agricultural development in Venezuela.

Above: **Fish being dried**

Left: **In the Maracaibo basin, cattle are driven to market.**

Laborers sort out the onion crop in the Lake Valencia basin.

VENEZUELAN WORKERS

The labor force in Venezuela is made up of about 7.4 million people, with an unemployment rate of almost 9%. About 6% work in financial and business services; 28% in community, social, and personal services; 10% in construction, electricity, gas, and water; 13% in agriculture, forestry, fishing, and mining; 22% in manufacturing, transport, and communications; and 21% in trade, including tourism. Nearly 62% of the workers are men.

The per capita income is about $3,000 a year. However, households are extremely large, so the purchasing power is quite low.

The working class structure in Venezuela is quite rigid. The upper-class people work mostly in business. Before the 20th century, this elite group made its money in agriculture. They owned large cocoa, sugar, or coffee plantations, using black and *mestizo* laborers. Now, many members of the upper class own family businesses.

The middle class has grown considerably since the discovery of petroleum and the subsequent creation of new jobs. Members of the middle class—most of them city dwellers—typically work in technology, business management, education, the priesthood, and the government. Most advertising is aimed at middle-class Venezuelans, as they are most likely to buy consumer goods and housing.

The lower class is mostly rural and makes up the majority of the population. Members of this class are often employed as subsistence farmers, day farm laborers, sharecroppers, domestic servants, or in other manual occupations.

In Caracas, members of the lower class often work in factories. Many work the night shift as well as the usual 40-hour week to make more money. Others work in the construction industry, which is based in Caracas. Many laborers belong to the Confederation of Venezuelan Workers, a trade union with more than 1.5 million members.

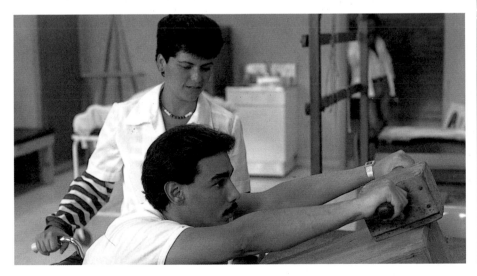

An occupational therapist in a hospital in Caracas, working with a young patient.

DOING BUSINESS IN VENEZUELA

The typical Venezuelan businessperson is usually male, quite sophisticated, well-educated, and accustomed to dealing with people from other countries and cultures. He works in a modern, air-conditioned office with the latest computers and fax machines, and wears a well-cut suit to work each day.

Venezuelan businesspeople are generally much more aware of office hierarchies than their American counterparts. They show respect for their superiors by holding the door for them, and they never interrupt or argue with them. Senior executives are always allowed to speak first at meetings and they are the decision-makers.

Business discussions are often formal. Venezuelans do not take kindly to impatient foreigners who fidget in their seat, dominate the conversation, or try to force the others into a quick decision. The typical Venezuelan businessman takes his time to assess the issues before voicing an idea. This way, he can back down or modify his position without drawing attention to himself.

Many Americans do business in quite a different fashion. They pay little attention to rank, they "get down to business" as soon as everybody is seated at the conference table, and they sell their products or ideas with great vigor and enthusiasm.

Venezuelans work hard, but they also believe in the old-fashioned Latin American siesta, or midday rest. The typical business day in Venezuela begins at 8:00 a.m. and ends at 6:00 p.m., Monday through Friday. There is a two-hour lunch break at noon and many people still go home for a large meal and a quick nap. Stores and banks are often closed between noon and 2:00 p.m., but restaurants usually stay open. Many people leave work early on Friday afternoons.

Opposite: **A view of Caracas. The Venezuelan capital, which is growing faster than any other Latin American capital, is the financial and business center of the country.**

VENEZUELANS

IN VENEZUELA, PEOPLE are unified by language, religion, and loyalty to their country, rather than separated by skin color. *Venezolanos* ("beh-neh-zoh-LAH-nohs") can be blue-eyed, blond-haired people of German ancestry or dark-eyed, dark-haired descendants of Indians. Last names range from the expected Martinezes and Pérezes to the more European-sounding Jordans and Vollmars.

Opposite and below:
Mestizos and blacks are two of the many races living in Venezuela.

Venezuelans have intermarried racially since colonial times. The majority (70%) are *mestizos* (people of mixed blood). *Mestizos* live throughout the country, in both urban and rural areas. White people of European descent (mostly Spanish and German) make up 20% of the population. They live mainly in cities. Blacks descended from people of African origin brought over as slaves make up 8% of the population, and native Indians the remaining 2%. Most blacks live in the northern coastal regions, while Indians live in the south or on the Colombian border.

About 2% of the people are legal immigrants of foreign birth. The number of illegal immigrants is difficult to assess; estimates range from 600,000 to 1.2 million. Most are Colombians who work in the construction industry in Caracas or in the petroleum industry in Maracaibo.

POPULATION DISTRIBUTION

In July 1992, there were more than 20.6 million people living in Venezuela. The country experienced a population boom in the 1920s, after the discovery of petroleum in Maracaibo, and again in the 1950s. After World War II, the prospect of wealth and jobs attracted more than 500,000 European immigrants from Italy, Spain, Portugal, France, Poland, and Germany.

Venezuelan oil wealth has given the people better health care services, which has helped to lower the country's death rate and maintain the high birth rate. In the 1930s, the annual death rate was 18 in 1,000; in 1992 it had dropped to four in 1,000. Life expectancy is about 73 years, and most people now die of more "modern" diseases such as heart disease, rather than the infections and contagious diseases that still kill large numbers of people in less developed countries.

Below: **College students in a park in Mérida**

Opposite: **A group of Orinoco Indians, at home under a makeshift shelter, some resting in hammocks.**

The annual rate of population growth was 3.6% in the 1960s and 2.6% in 1990. Despite this decrease, due to family planning encouraged by the government, the growth rate is still extremely high, with an estimated annual growth of 2.1% in the 1990s.

According to the 1990 census, 89% of Venezuelans now live in cities and towns with populations of more than 1,000 people, while only 9% live in the rural areas. All the population increases have been in the cities. The population of the vast rural areas remains a small 1.9 million people, making Venezuela one of the Western Hemisphere's least densely populated countries.

CLASS STRUCTURE

A deep-rooted class structure existed in Venezuela for centuries. For many years, Venezuela had only two classes: the whites, who were rich, and the rest of the population.

Today, wealth, family history, and cultural accomplishments determine the minority upper class. Their background is European, and many of them are well-educated and well-traveled. The women are very elegant. Few of them pursue careers, and most have household servants.

The middle class is made up of educated people of mixed ethnic backgrounds who are said to be racially tolerant. Much of their social life revolves around their occupations.

Manual laborers and the farmers who live in both the urban and rural areas make up the lower class. They often live in small villages in the country and tend to be closely-knit. Social life revolves around planting, harvesting, and religious ceremonies.

As in many Latin American countries, in Venezuela there is a tremendous gap between rich and poor. In February 1990, some 300 people were killed in riots in Caracas after the government announced a plan to raise gas prices and bus fares.

"The poor man knows how poor he is. He has his transistor radio."

—*ex-President Pérez*

GERMANY IN VENEZUELA

In the 1830s, after the wars that stripped the countryside of farmers and slave workers, the Venezuelan government encouraged people from Europe to migrate to Venezuela. An Italian geographer and a German mapmaker came up with an idea to send a colony of German peasants to an area near Caracas where they could settle down and hopefully prosper. The land belonged to a wealthy aristocrat named Manuel Felipe de Tovar, but he donated it to the colony and Colonia Tovar was settled.

A school, church, and pharmacy were soon built, and a printing press was brought in to publish the news in Spanish and German. The German mapmaker, Alexander Benitz, recruited people from the Black Forest in Germany. He wished to make the colony completely self-sufficient, so he chose artisans, doctors, teachers, and farmers. A group of 374 men, women, and children set out for Venezuela in 1843. Unfortunately, 70 of them died of smallpox aboard ship.

The remaining colonists landed on an open beach and, since there were no roads leading to the colony, had to climb the mountains up to Colonia Tovar on foot. More died along the way, but the survivors found a gloriously beautiful place with a perfect climate waiting for them. They soon settled down and waited for more of their countrymen to join them. Unfortunately, none came, and the German immigrants were forgotten by the Venezuelan government. They remained isolated, intermarried, and retained the German language and customs they had brought with them. Amazingly enough, they remained this way for more than 80 years, until they were rediscovered about 40 years ago when a good road was built from Caracas.

Now Colonia Tovar is a popular tourist attraction. People come from all over Venezuela to view Bavarian-style buildings, eat German sausage, sauerkraut, Black Forest cake and homemade jam, and watch authentic German dancing by blond, blue-eyed German Venezuelans.

THE INDIANS OF VENEZUELA

The Venezuelan Indian population has been decreasing steadily since the early 16th century. Today, the Carib- and Arawak-speaking tribes number only between 200,000 and 400,000. Many of them live in the most inaccessible areas: the Orinoco Delta, the rain forests that spread south to Brazil and west to Colombia, and the desert-like area of the Guajira Peninsula, just north of Maracaibo.

A Warau Indian prepares palm fibers to weave a hammock.

The Guajiro Indians are a very interesting group. They speak their own language, wear distinctive, colorful clothes, and follow ancient customs and rituals. Yet some have left their desert homes for jobs in Maracaibo and have assimilated quite easily into urban life. Some work in the oil and construction industries and others sell fruits and vegetables at the outdoor markets.

Those who stay on the Guajira Peninsula are semi-nomadic, leaving their homes in search of water and food for themselves and their cattle. Although many Guajiros have married people of other races, their Indian culture is strong, and many children of mixed marriages think of themselves as Guajiros rather than *mestizos*. Often

Left and below: **Indians of Zulia State** (*left*) **and the Orinoco Delta** (*below*).

Guajiros who are educated in the city return to the land to adopt their former dress and way of life.

At least 12 different Indian tribes live in the Amazonas Federal Territory near the Brazilian border. Each has its own language and culture. The Makiritare, or Yekuana people, live on rivers and use 54-foot-long dugout canoes that they make from tree trunks for transport. The Piaroa build 36-foot-high conical houses thatched with palm fronds. The warlike Yanomami (who also live in Brazil) are one of the most isolated tribes in Venezuela and many of the people have never seen a white man or woman. Warau Indians live in the Orinoco River delta. They are skilled fishermen and navigators and build their homes on stilts.

DRESS HABITS

In Caracas and other large cities, upper- and upper-middle-class people dress conservatively, the way Americans and Europeans do: suits, white shirts, and ties for men; dresses, skirts and blouses, or suits for women. Women do not wear stockings, however, except for the most formal occasions. Businesswomen wear makeup and dress elegantly, with jewelry and high heels, but they never wear revealing clothing. At night, people dress rather formally for dining out or going to the theater: jackets and ties for men and cocktail dresses (often with designer labels) for women. Men wear jackets even to pizza parlors in Caracas! Nice jeans and stylish casual clothing are worn on the streets. Shorts are frowned upon, except at the beach or on the tennis court. Few people wear hats.

The working-class city dwellers usually wear inexpensive cotton clothes: men are often seen in light-colored shirts open at the neck, paired with khaki pants; women wear print dresses, skirts, and blouses.

Some small children go naked in the poorest sections, but are nicely dressed for church on Sundays, as parents take pride in how their children look. Girl toddlers often wear brightly-colored ruffled dresses to Mass. Many of the little girls have their ears pierced and wear gold jewelry. All children wear uniforms to school.

In the rural areas, men often wear straw hats in hot weather and felt ones in cooler weather. Lower-class men often wear pants cut off at the knees and sandals or no shoes. Upper-class men wear boots or shoes, but rarely dress in formal jackets and ties.

Holidays in the lowlands find men wearing traditional *liquiliqui* ("lih-

Above: **Venezuelan students from Valencia, in modern dress.**

Opposite top: **Fashion must suit the climate. Here a Guajiro Indian wears black face paint to protect her complexion from salt and sun.**

Opposite bottom: **At a Federation meeting, hats and open-neck shirts are respectable attire.**

kih-LIH-kih"), white cotton shirt and pants fastened with leather or gold buttons or a sash. Women wear colorful full skirts called *joroperas* ("hoh-roh-PAY-rahs") with elaborately embroidered off-the-shoulder blouses.

Guajiro Indian women wear flowing, floor-length *mantas* ("MAHN-tahs") in stunning colors; men often wear only a shirt, loincloth, and straw hat. Guajiros are excellent weavers of brightly-colored belts and saddlebags.

LIFESTYLE

DESPITE THE FACT that Venezuela is a land of extreme contrasts, there is a distinct Venezuelan personality. To understand the Venezuelan way of life, it is important to know how Venezuelans live, how they spend their days, and how they interact with each other.

HOUSING

The diversity of Venezuelan culture is nowhere more evident than in the living conditions of Venezuelans. The people of Venezuela have extremely different worlds: those who live in the cities versus those who live in the country; apartment dwellers versus slum dwellers; rich versus poor.

Contrasts in housing are particularly apparent in the big cities, especially Caracas, which suffers from an acute housing shortage. During periods of economic growth, people have flocked to the capital in search of jobs. Many have found employment, but few have found affordable housing. Now, although one in every five Venezuelans lives in Caracas, more than one-third of them live in slums.

Only the wealthiest *caraqueños* live in single-family homes. These are usually spacious, with gardens, swimming pools, and balconies. The wealthy often have beach homes as well as apartments in North America.

Most of the middle class and the upper class live in high-rise apartment buildings. The typical apartment is equipped with bedrooms, a kitchen, a bathroom, a living room, and a balcony. The nicer buildings have swimming pools. Many upper-middle-class apartments have servants' quarters.

Housing costs in Caracas are extremely high, comparable to New York, Tokyo, or Rio. Although the government has constructed some public housing, the demand still far exceeds the supply. Hence, the poorest *caraqueños* have had to build shanties on the hilly outskirts of the city where they can live rent-free.

Opposite: **Venezuelan schoolboys of Coro in front of a mural**

Apartment blocks and shanties of Caracas. Some shanties are made of wooden planks and corrugated iron roofs. Once shanty dwellers have weatherproofed their homes, they often buy television sets and refrigerators. Electricity may be brought in by connecting wires to the transmission lines.

SPANISH ARCHITECTURAL ROOTS

Many Venezuelan homes have a distinctly Spanish look. The house is surrounded by a wall to protect the residents' privacy. Rooms are built around a patio that is often filled with brightly-colored flowers and plants. Roofs are made from traditional dark-brown Spanish tiles, and the walls—both outside and inside—are painted in vibrant colors like lemon yellow, fuchsia, or emerald green.

RANCHOS

Ranchos, or shanties, are also found in the rural areas. There, however, the walls are made from poles or bamboo, overlaid with palm fronds or mud. The roof is thatched with palm fronds and the floor is dirt. Kerosene lamps provide artificial light and water is often brought in from a nearby stream or well. Most of these homes have only two rooms: the kitchen and the living room/bedroom. Oil- or wood-burning stoves are used in the kitchen.

Instead of beds, *rancho* dwellers often use hammocks, or *chinchorros* ("chin-CHOR-rohs"), which are both comfortable and easily stored. These are hung by large hooks in the walls. Sometimes, the sleeping area is shared by pets or even livestock like chickens, goats, and pigs. Rooms are easily added to the *rancho* as the family grows.

In many small towns, buildings are laid out according to a pattern brought over centuries ago by the Spanish colonists. Government and religious buildings border the town's central plaza, and all the streets are laid out rectangularly, in an effort to achieve balance and harmony. In colonial times, the central plaza was the marketplace. It was flanked by the most important public buildings and the houses of the town's most important citizens. Houses of government officials and business-men were just off the square. The lowest class of people lived the farthest away from the plaza. This was the plan throughout the Spanish New World.

A typical upper-class bungalow in Caracas. Notice that there is a name as well as a number on the house.

THE FAMILY UNIT

In Venezuela, the family unit is more important than any of its individual constituents. Family members feel closer to and more trusting of each other than of any outsiders. The father is king of the household; the mother is queen of domestic issues; and the children are to respect and revere

A three-generation Venezuelan family

both. Often, grandparents are part of the household, and they too are treated with respect. Even when the children grow up, marry, and move away, they maintain close contact with their families and come home when they are needed.

In many Latin American cultures, the family circle is extended through the appointment of godparents for the children. These *comadres* ("kom-MAH-drays," literally "co-mothers") and *compadres* ("kom-PAH-drays," or "co-fathers") are supposed to ensure their godchildren's religious and moral education. Parents usually ask only close friends whom they trust and admire to be their children's godparents. Often, godparents act as sponsors for their godchildren; they contribute money toward their First Communion ceremony, for instance, or help them make connections in later life when they wish to seek employment.

THE VENEZUELAN MAN AND HIS LLANERO

The typical Venezuelan man is traditional in outlook. He makes the decisions at home; he is the chief—and often the sole—wage earner. He prefers that his wife not work, as this implies he cannot provide adequately for the family. Venezuelan men—and Venezuelans in general—are quite conscious of the image they present to society. They would never wish to appear weak or unmasculine, or dominated by their wives.

The typical Venezuelan man regards the cowboy of the *llanos*, or the *llanero*, as his hero. In the sparsely populated central region of Venezuela, where floods alternate with drought, the *llanero* is famed for his courage and strength. Traditionally, the *llanero* worked extremely hard. He drank nothing but a cup of strong coffee in the morning, and then spent his day on a half-wild horse, rounding up his herd with his lasso, and driving it to be branded. In the wet season, he would follow his cattle in a canoe; in the dry season, he would drive them across the plains in a cloud of heat and dust. After an exhausting day, the *llanero* of Venezuelan folklore would sit by the fire with his companions and talk of the events of the day. Then he would eat a hearty meal and, accompanied by his four-stringed guitar, the *cuatro* ("KWAH-troh"), sing verses about the suffering of the Indians or the suppressed African slaves, and dance traditional Venezuelan dances. At the end of the day, he would hang his hammock on a hook and sleep off his physical exhaustion, only to begin again at sunrise.

The llanero*'s existence is a solitary one; his motto was: "I, on my horse, above me my hat, above my hat, God." He was free and indomitable, and lived by muscle and the determination to battle nature.*

Right and opposite: **The typical Venezuelan woman sees herself as a traditional homemaker. Her children are her main concern. In the cities, however, women are being trained to move into technical and professional jobs. Pictured here are a family from the Guayana region and students in a chemistry laboratory of a university in Mérida.**

THE TRADITIONAL VENEZUELAN WOMAN

Venezuelan women—like most Latin American women—tend to be conservative, at least by American standards. It was not too long ago that a woman would not appear in public unless she was accompanied by a chaperone. Many Latin American women still do not go out alone at night, or even in groups of women. They are often escorted by their brothers or fathers, who act as their protectors.

The typical Latin American woman is likely to dress conventionally. She may not assert her personality or put forth her ideas readily in public, but she does have considerable power within the home.

Most Latin American women—from every social class—desire to get married and raise children. Within the home, they see themselves as administrators whose job it is to oversee the household budget, the children's religious upbringing, the social activities, and the housework. Children treat their mothers with unreserved affection; they are often not as openly affectionate with their fathers, who act as the family disciplinarians.

Wives and mothers are very concerned with cleanliness, in the home and with regard to personal appearance. They bathe their children two or three times a day, and change them into freshly washed and pressed clothes for dinner. (Working men and women come home at siesta time to eat, nap, bathe, and change.)

THE WORKING WOMAN

Economic development and urbanization have brought about employment opportunities for women. More women than men have moved from rural areas to the cities in recent years, and they have found a broader range of jobs open to them, including domestic and factory work.

More women have also begun entering the professional and technical fields. They are becoming doctors, lawyers, dentists, architects, teachers, nurses, and laboratory technicians. The percentage of working women was 38.5% of all workers in 1990. Women have also made some inroads into Venezuelan politics: more than a dozen women have served in the Chamber of Deputies, and the first woman presidential candidate, Ismenia Villaba, ran in the 1989 election.

Women of the upper class often devote themselves to charitable causes such as adult literacy programs, or cultural institutions, such as museums and ballet companies. It is prestigious for them to go to college, even if they have no intention of working after graduation. In Venezuela, more than 50% of the students enrolled in universities in 1990 were women.

When they have achieved a certain amount of professional success or independence, Venezuelan women choose to preserve their femininity by not appearing overly aggressive or competitive.

A Venezuelan boy takes a break at the marketplace in Ciudad Bolívar.

VENEZUELAN CHILDREN

Most Venezuelan infants are pampered, whether they are born into upper-class or lower-class families. Small children are given lots of attention by all members of the extended family. Rarely are they disciplined. Little girls are encouraged to be motherly toward their younger siblings and to be more passive when dealing with little boys. As children grow, girls are watched more closely than their brothers, who are given fewer responsibilities and more freedom.

EDUCATION IN VENEZUELA

In the past, only upper-class Venezuelans were educated. School was thought to be unnecessary for the others, who pursued careers in manual labor. Rómulo Betancourt's government, which took office in 1959, was the first to take education seriously. Results became apparent almost immediately. New schools were built all over the country, educational material was brought in, and teacher-training programs were developed. In just five years, some 2,287 new schools were built.

Today, about 15% of children attend private, church-related primary and secondary schools; 75% of the rest go to schools that are directly administered by the ministry of education in Caracas. Public education—from kindergarten through university—is free.

It is compulsory to attend primary school until the age of 14. Primary school subjects are much like their U.S. counterparts: reading, writing, arithmetic, Spanish, natural science, history, geography, and civics. Some children in the remotest areas have only a one-room schoolhouse with an undertrained teacher or no school at all.

After six years of primary school, students attend a four-year program in science and the humanities. A second program, including philosophy, literature, physical science, mathematics, and biology, prepares them for college. Secondary school students can attend technical schools for instruction in industry and commerce, the trades, nursing, and social welfare. The government also administers extensive adult literacy and job-training programs. As a result, the literacy rate has risen.

About 450 students are enrolled in university programs. Most of them study economics, business, law, health, and engineering. Leading public universities include the Central University of Venezuela, founded in 1725, Los Andes University, and Simón Bolívar University.

Total school enrollment in 1958 was 845,000; by 1989, it was nearly three million. The literacy rate, which was just over 50% in the 1950s, reached 82% by the 1970s and 92.2% by 1990.

SOCIAL GRACES

Major Venezuelan cities have become more internationally focused since the oil boom and the subsequent influx of foreigners and their customs. The United States in particular has made a significant impact on Venezuelan society, but not so much that Venezuelans—especially those of the upper classes—have given up their social rituals.

Venezuelan society is essentially hierarchical: rank is very important. Older people come before younger people; people with titles wield more influence than those without; members of the upper class might be served in a restaurant before the middle-class diners who got there first. When somebody has a title—doctor, professor, lawyer—it is important to use it when addressing him or her.

Receiving an invitation to a Venezuelan home is considered something of an honor. The home is a refuge, a place where only the extended family and the closest friends are welcome. Guests who fall into neither of these categories are treated formally. In a small party, the guest is introduced by the host or hostess and is expected to shake hands with, greet, and say goodbye to each of the other guests individually. The general "hi, everybody" and universal "take care" that Americans arrive and depart with would be considered undignified at a Venezuelan get-together. At large gatherings, guests introduce themselves.

Certain subjects of conversation are taboo at dinner parties, especially for foreigners. It is considered impolite to gossip or spread rumors about well-known personalities, to discuss politics, to tell political jokes, or to talk about the problem of illegal aliens from Colombia. Controversial subjects are not raised, as arguing must be avoided at all costs. Venezuelans do not like to be asked personal questions—about marriage or family, for instance—until they know the person fairly well.

Venezuelans still follow the custom of making social calls. These are to admire a new baby or a new house, or even to thank a host or hostess for an invitation to dinner a few days previously. People do not call on each other between 1:00 p.m. and 4:00 p.m., however, as this is siesta time, when people nap, read, or write letters. In the United States, neighbors often drop in on a newcomer to welcome him or her to the area. In Venezuela, it is just the opposite: newcomers call on the established members of the community to introduce themselves.

In Venezuela, a cup of coffee is the symbol of hospitality. It is offered during the social call, after dinner, or at the start of a business meeting. It is considered rude to decline a cup of coffee, but it is acceptable to drink only one or two sips.

A sidewalk café in Caracas. Venezuelans are more likely to entertain someone they know only casually at a club or restaurant. There is no such thing as "going Dutch" in Venezuela; the person who invites pays for the meal. When a man and a woman dine together, the man never lets the woman pay.

63

TAKING TIME

Venezuelans like to take their time. If they arrive late for an appointment, it might be because they were taking time to be courteous at a previous meeting. Venezuelans take a more relaxed attitude toward tardiness than most people. In Caracas, where traffic jams are common, delays are considered a part of life, and *caraqueños* accept them casually, even cheerfully. When entering an office or shop, it is more important to stop and greet the receptionist or the shopkeeper than to rush about accomplishing something. A smile or a nod is all that is required.

In business, Venezuelans take their time to assess the situation before offering an idea or making a decision. Personal relationships also progress slowly and carefully. Venezuelans are not likely to appreciate the impatient businessman who demands an immediate answer or an acquaintance who asks intimate questions.

Americans use the phone, the memo, or the fax to hurry things along. This leaves no time for courtesies, cups of coffee, and careful examination of the matters at hand. Venezuelan businessmen much prefer to meet. Though it takes more time, it is more personal.

THE VENEZUELAN LIFE CYCLE

Because Venezuela is essentially a Roman Catholic country and customs are derived from the Spanish culture, most of the significant life events—birth, puberty, marriage, and death—are outwardly similar to the customs of any country whose main religion is Roman Catholicism. There are differences, however, which give meaningful insights into the Venezuelan personality.

THE NEW BABY As in many other societies, the birth of a child in Venezuela is a time of great rejoicing. Relatives and close family friends flock to the home of the newborn to celebrate the arrival in style. Traditionally, older people bring a strong homemade liquor to toast the baby's health.

In general, boys are preferred, because girls require more supervision, and when they get married, more money. People of the upper classes often choose to have big families with eight or nine children. Extremely poor families sometimes have even more than that. Most middle-class couples are well informed about family planning and opt for small families with only two or three children.

In 1992, the birth rate was 27 in 1,000.

Venezuelan girls are introduced early to the art of femininity.

All eyes are turned expectantly on the *piñata.*

CHILDREN'S PARTIES The highlight of children's birthday parties in Venezuela is often the *piñata* ("pih-NYAH-tah"), a brightly-colored figure in the shape of a man or an animal that is stuffed with toys and candy. The children are blindfolded and given a stick; they take turns trying to hit the *piñata* until it opens up and the loot inside falls out. In Venezuela there are entire shops that carry nothing but *piñatas* and their contents.

THE 15TH BIRTHDAY PARTY When Venezuelan girls reach the age of 15, many have a *quinceañera* ("kin-seh-ah-nih-AIR-rah"), or a special 15th birthday party. This ritual, a Latin form of the debutante or "coming out" party, is common in many Latin American cultures. It announces to society that she is now a woman and ready to join the social world. In the past, the *quinceañera's* purpose was to bring the girl into contact with marriageable men, but this purpose has become obsolete in modern Latin American countries.

The expense scale varies: poorer families might invite a hundred or so guests while wealthy families have been known to invite thousands. Most parties are held in clubs or halls, or for wealthy families, in the home. The larger celebrations can cost a great deal and can put the family in debt for years.

The party begins at about 9:00 p.m. and can last until dawn, but usually ends at about 2:00 a.m. Dinner and drinks are served, although the birthday girl is usually only allowed a sip of champagne from her father's glass. For dessert, there is usually a large cake (in wealthy families it is multi-tiered like a wedding cake).

Girls often wear very fancy ball gowns, and men wear either nice suits or tuxedos. There is often a band, and the girl traditionally dances the first dance (which is likely to be a waltz) with her father. Then she dances with her male peers. It is considered a status symbol to give a fancy *quinceañera*. In the big cities, the party will often be described in the newspapers.

THE WEDDING Wedding parties are often grand affairs as well. Like *quinceañeras*, they give Venezuelans a chance to invite a great many guests and to show society that they spare no expense in celebrating the marriage of their daughter. Among the upper classes, it is considered good luck if the bride and groom can sneak away from the wedding celebration within a few hours of its commencement without being noticed.

THE FUNERAL Funerals in Venezuela are serious occasions. Often, after the ceremony, family members gather at the home of the bereaved to comfort them. The wife of a deceased man will usually wear black for a long time if she is a religious woman. Some widows even wear black for the rest of their lives. Less traditional or younger widows are not likely to wear black at all. Widowers, on the other hand, often adopt dark dress for a week or a month.

Many of the customs and attitudes of the Venezuelans in the 20th century can be traced back through the 19th century to the colonial period.

67

RELIGION

THE OFFICIAL RELIGION OF Venezuela is Catholicism, but the 1961 constitution guarantees freedom of religion. In 1990, 95% of the population was Catholic; 2% Protestant; and the rest Jewish, Muslim, Baha'i, Buddhist, tribal religionist, Afro-American spiritualist, or simply atheist.

The Spanish brought Catholicism to Venezuela. In 1513, Dominican and Franciscan priests came to northeastern Venezuela to develop coffee, sugar, and cocoa plantations and to teach native Indians about cattle breeding. Capuchin missionaries founded 100 stations in the *llanos* between 1658 and 1758, while Jesuits were active in the Orinoco River areas. They were quite successful in their conversion attempts and in building and running religious schools throughout the country.

Although the Catholic Church is not formally linked to the state, it is subsidized by the government, which pays the salaries of some church officials and helps maintain the churches themselves. The government is consulted when powerful church officials are named, and church representatives often attend important functions like the opening of a power plant. Since the Vatican appointed the first Venezuelan cardinal in 1960, the country has seen much missionary work.

Venezuela has many beautiful Catholic churches. There is at least one in each town. Many are modeled after the Cathedral of Coro on the Caribbean coast, and La Asuncíon on Margarita Island, both completed in 1617. Architectural ornamentation is minimal.

Opposite: **Inside the Cathedral of Maracay**

Above: **Vendors wait for their customers outside the Cathedral of Mérida.**

69

Opposite: **The tiled floor and pews in the church of San Francisco, near Maracaibo, are typical of the Catholic churches in Venezuela.**

CATHOLIC BELIEFS AND TRADITIONS

Roman Catholics believe that the Pope is the supreme leader of the Church. He is thought to be the successor to St. Peter, the disciple of Jesus Christ, who was the first pope, or "father" on earth. Regarding matters of faith, the Pope is said to be infallible. In the Roman Catholic Church, followers should perform six of the following seven sacraments, or actions to achieve grace, or be admitted to heaven.

1. BAPTISM An infant is baptized to be cleansed of the "original sin," or spirit of disobedience with which it is born. (According to Christian belief, everyone is born with Adam and Eve's sin of disobedience.) Baptism gives the infant a fresh start and allows it to become a member of the Church. The act is performed by a priest who pours water over the forehead and says, "I baptize you in the name of the Father and of the Son and of the Holy Spirit."

In Venezuela, a child's baptism is a very important occasion. It is done by members of all classes, in both rural and urban areas. Those who live in remote areas of the country away from parish centers will travel long distances to have their infants baptized. Poorer parents will wait until they can raise enough money for a proper christening party, or choose a set of godparents who are willing to contribute. In wealthier families, christening parties can be elaborate affairs.

2. CONFIRMATION Young people are confirmed between the ages of 12 and 18, although they can be younger or older. Confirmation is an act that confirms or seals the faith given to the child at baptism. It indicates that the person is now an adult and is responsible for his or her own religious life.

3. HOLY EUCHARIST This ritual is also called the blessed sacrament. Catholics believe that Christ himself exists in the holy bread and wine that are consecrated on the church altar. By ingesting the bread and wine, the receiver is nourished spiritually. The first part of a Catholic Mass consists of recitations from the scriptures, and the second of taking the Holy Eucharist.

Children receive their First Communion when they are about 7 years old and are considered to know the difference between right and wrong. Before receiving the sacrament, they are expected to be "worthy," or in a spirit of prayer. They are not to eat for one hour before the ceremony.

4. PENANCE This ritual entails confessing one's sins to a priest, who sits out of sight in a confessional, a box-like cubicle inside the church. Only what are termed "mortal sins"—those that separate people from God or put them in opposition to God—need to be confessed. The priest forgives the sinners and asks them to perform certain prayers or rituals to atone for their sins and ease their punishment.

5. MATRIMONY To Catholics, marriage is a sacred event that allows a couple to have children. Marriages should not be broken by divorce. Divorce does happen in Venezuela, however.

6. ANOINTING THE SICK This ritual is used only for the very sick or dying. Also known as performing the "last rites," this sacrament brings forgiveness to the dying and prepares them for entry into heaven. The priest puts olive oil—

Above and opposite: **Outside the church in the German immigrant settlement of Colonia Tovar, before Sunday Mass. Note the dress and features of the people.**

a symbol of light, strength, and life—on the forehead of the dying person and asks for forgiveness for sins committed by each of the senses: sight, touch, taste, smell, and hearing.

7. HOLY ORDERS This sacrament applies only to priests. It is performed by a bishop, who lays his hands on the candidate for priesthood and gives him the power to perform the Holy Eucharist and to forgive sins. Only men can be priests in the Catholic Church; they take a vow of celibacy, promising that they will not marry. The priesthood has various categories: a monsignor performs special duties in a Catholic community; a bishop is in charge of a diocese, or the Catholics in a city and the surrounding areas; an archbishop serves a large city; and a cardinal is an archbishop appointed by the Pope as an adviser. One of the most significant jobs of a cardinal is to elect a new pope.

Interior of Barquisimeto
Cathedral, designed by
Jan Berg Kemp

ATTITUDES TOWARD CATHOLICISM

Although most Venezuelans consider themselves Catholic, religion does not have a significant influence on their daily lives. Of the whole population, 95% are nominally Catholic, but only 25% are practicing Catholics. Generally, only the elderly actually attend church daily and offer prayers before each meal. Most younger people attend church only on festive religious occasions such as Christmas, weddings, baptisms, or saints' days. For them, the social atmosphere often takes precedence over the religious significance of the ceremony.

Venezuelan women tend to be more religious than the men. They are responsible for the moral and religious education of their children, especially the girls. From adolescence, boys are not encouraged to be religious, as devotion is not considered a masculine trait. This may be why the Catholic Church has difficulty recruiting priests from among the Venezuelan male population. Although about half the nuns in the country are Venezuelans, a great majority of priests come from Spain.

Members of the middle class have historically been more religious than those of the other classes and priests usually come from the middle class.

Catholics in the rural states of Mérida, Táchira, and Trujillo, where

THE CULT OF MARÍA LIONZA

María Lionza, the goddess of nature and fertility, and protector of forests, wild animals, and mineral wealth, is worshiped by all social classes in Venezuela, although she is particularly popular among the urban poor. The cult of María Lionza is a mixture of Indian, African, and Christian beliefs and practices. She has elements of the Arawak water goddess, West African mythological figures, and the Virgin Mary.

Legend has it that María Lionza was a beautiful Indian girl who disappeared in the forest and was never seen again, except as a spirit. She is said to live with her servants in a golden palace surrounded by wild animals in the Sorte Mountains of Yaracuy. She rides on the back of a tapir, a gentle beast considered sacred by some Indian tribes.

During a cult service, a priest calls up spirits and deities that possess mediums. The spirits are consulted for advice and assistance. Tobacco smoke is used as a cure, to ward off evil spirits, and to bring about spiritual cleansing.

María Lionza is associated with popular Catholic saints, a historical figure named Negro Miguel who instigated an uprising among the slaves, and even Simón Bolívar, the Venezuelan liberator. In the Sorte Mountains, there are countless images of the goddess. In the ceremonies that take place there, candles burn everywhere and worshipers often appear barefoot, to maintain contact with the earth. They never stand with arms or hands crossed, as this is said to bring bad luck.

Although the worship of María Lionza takes many different forms throughout the country, an attempt at solidarity was made in 1968 when the groups were legalized as a society under the name of the Aboriginal Cult of María Lionza, headquartered in Caracas.

agricultural traditions have been maintained, seem to be more serious about their faith. Urban stress often leaves little time for spiritual development.

FOLK BELIEFS AND SUPERSTITIONS

For special favors, people ask St. Anthony for help. They tie down a small statue of him and refuse to untie it until the favor is granted.

Folk beliefs based on the occult are common throughout Venezuela, especially in remote rural areas. These too combine Catholic practices with those of African and Indian faiths. In the Andes, some people believe that physical objects—like water—can contain supernatural powers. People of all ethnic origins seek the advice of resident faith healers. Many native Indians, especially among the Arawak and Carib tribes, believe in the powers of spiritualists.

Venezuelans are a superstitious people in general. Many believe in witches and demons that take human form to offer temptations. *Anima solas* ("ah-NEE-mah SOH-lahs"), or "lost souls," are said to make occasional appearances; they are best diffused by covering one's face and praying aloud. Other spirits take animal forms.

In Venezuela, Tuesday the 13th rather than Friday the 13th is said to be unlucky. North American superstitions about walking under ladders and letting black cats cross your path are also heeded by Venezuelans. For good luck a polished seed of a tropical tree is as good as a rabbit's foot. The seed can be given as a gift, stolen, or found, but it must never be bought.

Some Venezuelans consider it bad luck to be given handkerchiefs, a seashell, a live snake, or something made from snakeskin. Others consider a rattlesnake tail to be a symbol of good luck. If the palm of your right hand itches, then somebody owes you money; if it is in the left hand, then *you* owe money. When you open a bottle of rum, you are supposed to spill a few drops on the ground in order to give the dead a taste. In Venezuela, if you dream about a snake, it means that somebody is gossiping about you; but if in the dream you behead the snake, that indicates that you have stopped the gossip from spreading.

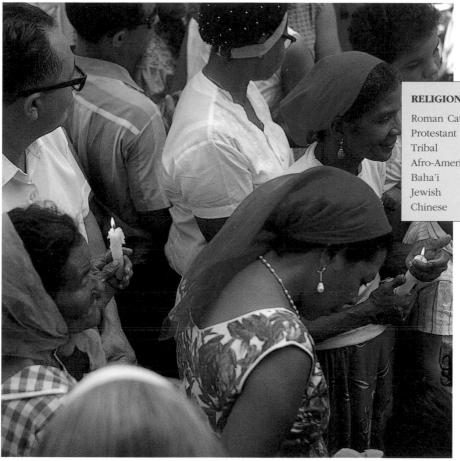

RELIGION AND VENEZUELANS*

Roman Catholic	17,650,000
Protestant	240,000
Tribal	212,000
Afro-American spiritualist	122,000
Baha'i	35,000
Jewish	12,000
Chinese	6,000

* 400,000 Catholics also profess to be followers of the cult of María Lionza. Tribal religions are religions of native Indians. Afro-American spiritualists are those who do not classify themselves as Christians. Source: *World Christian Encyclopedia*, Oxford University Press, 1982.

OTHER RELIGIONS

The Baha'i and Protestant faiths have experienced rapid growth in Venezuela in recent years. Both have converted many members from the Guajiro tribe.

Judaism is represented by both Sephardic groups, who came from Spain, and Ashkenazi groups, who emigrated from central and eastern Europe after World War II. The oldest Jewish cemetery in Latin America is located at Coro.

There are also several Greek and Ukrainian Orthodox congregations in Venezuela, as well as followers of Buddhism.

GALERIAS 1.890
SU CENTRO COMERCIAL

El Regalo Dorado

LA MODA **Kuroki** DEL JAPON

juanma **BOUTIQUE**

Fantasías Nathalí
BROCHES-ZARCILLOS-COLLARES
ELABORACION - MATERIALES
CURSOS

CURIOSIARTE *Artesania*

Tia Nicota
Salon de té
Dulcería
Bombonería

HINDU

FOTOCOPIAS
TRANSCRIPCION DE TEXTOS Loc. 8

Génesis DISEÑOS

Cautxras REGALOS

NINA **BOUTIQUE S.R.L.** LOCAL 11

LANGUAGE

THE OFFICIAL LANGUAGE of Venezuela is Spanish, as it is in most of South America. (Portuguese is spoken in Brazil, and French, English, and Dutch in Guyana.) The level of Spanish is standard throughout Venezuela's educated population, but varies from region to region among the less educated.

People from the Andean states of Mérida, Trujillo, and Táchira, who are said to be conservative, speak with a refined accent. In Maracaibo, people accentuate their syllables clearly, while inhabitants of Cumaná or Margarita Island speak fast. The *llaneros* have a distinct accent, as do the inhabitants of Coro and Caracas. Yet everybody can understand everybody else.

"VENEZUELANISMS"

People of all classes and ethnic groups are familiar with many distinctly Venezuelan words. These are drawn from numerous African and Indian languages that have crept into the culture, and some have Spanish origins. Some Indian words that have found their way into the mainstream include *hamaca* ("ah-MAH-kah," hammock), *barbacao* ("bar-bah-KAH-oh," barbecue), and *tabaco* ("tah-BAH-koh," tobacco), all from the Arawak language; and *butaca* ("boo-TAH-kah," theater stall), from the Cumanagoto language. Of course, some of these have been incorporated into English as well.

Opposite: **Despite the pervasive influence of English, shop signs are all in Spanish.**

Below: **Going to the movies is a favorite activity of Venezuelans.**

MADE IN VENEZUELA

Chevere	("chair-BAY-ray") This is the Venezuelan equivalent of "wow" or "great"; people who use it are almost immediately recognizable as Venezuelans.
Que palo de agua!	("kay PAH-loh day AH-guah") Literally this means, "What a stick of water!" but it is used to mean, "What a rainstorm!"
Gordo or *Gorda*	("GOR-doh" or "GOR-dah") Literally "fat," but in Venezuela this is a term of affection and not to be taken as an offense.
Teleculebra	("tay-lay-koo-LAY-brah") In direct translation, this means "television snake," but it is used in Venezuela to describe a soap opera where the characters are greedy, lustful, or cunning.
Mas o menos	("mass oh MAY-noss") "More or less." In Venezuela, this might be used as an answer to "How are you?" ("Okay, not great") or "How much did it cost?" ("Not too much, not too little").
Que ganga!	("kay GAHNG-gah") "What a bargain!" This can be heard during or after one of the favorite pastimes in Venezuela: shopping.

Some "Venezuelanisms" of Spanish origin have been adapted to describe modern situations. In Caracas, which is renowned for its traffic jams, for instance, *caraqueños* have devised a vocabulary to describe various types of congestion: *galletas* ("gah-lih-AIR-tahs," basic traffic jams), *colas* ("KOH-lahs," long traffic jams that snake along slowly), and *trancas* (TRAHN-cahs," total blockages). *Vivos* ("BEE-bohs") are drivers who pay no attention to traffic laws and often cause accidents.

AMERICAN INFLUENCE

Venezuelans who travel regularly or who come in contact with people from other cultures speak English as well as other languages (Portuguese, French, German, and Italian, for example). There are also substantial immigrant populations whose first language is Portuguese or Italian.

English has been creeping steadily into the language, especially in urban areas, because of the influx of expatriate North Americans employed in the petroleum industry. In the areas of sports and recreation, the

influence of the *yanqui* ("YAHN-kih") is clear. In the national sport of baseball (in Venezuela, it is called *beisbol,* "beh-EES-bol"), for instance, "ball one" is *bol uán* ("bol OO-wan"), "ball two" is *bol tu* ("bol TOO"), "strike three" is *estrai tri* ("ess-TRAH-ee tree"), "struck out" is *estrocao* ("ess-troh-KAH-oh"), a "hit" is a *hit,* and "home run" is *jonrón* ("khon-RHON"). If these terms were translated directly into Spanish, of course, they would not sound nearly as American.

In the office and elsewhere, other Americanisms have been adopted wholeheartedly, as in "O.K." and *olrai* ("OHL-rah-ee," all right). A security guard or night watchman is called a *wachiman* ("wah-chih-MAHN"), a clutch in a standard shift car is a *croche* ("CROH-chay"), and when your gas tank reads "F," it is, in short, *full.*

Tourists in a hotel on the Caribbean coast. A working knowledge of English is an asset in service industries, particularly those related to tourism. However, many linguistic purists in Venezuela object to the importation of foreign words. Despite a law that requires all foreign advertising copy to be translated completely into Spanish, English words continue to assault the Venezuelan vocabulary.

In Caracas, teachers demonstrate for the literacy campaign.

A UNIFYING FORCE

The majority of Venezuelans speak only Spanish. This helps to unite the people, who see themselves more as *Venezolanos* than anything else. Although there are distinct words to define the different races, these terms are not racist. A *blanco* ("BLAHN-koh") is a white person; a *negro* ("NAY-groh") is a black person; a *mulatto* ("moo-LAHT-toh") is a racial mixture of black and white; a *pardo* ("PAR-doh") is someone of black, white, and Indian blood; a *zambo* ("ZAHM-boh") is a racial mix of Indian and black; and a *mestizo*, which used to mean someone of Indian and white heritage, has come to designate all forms of racial mixture.

INDIAN LANGUAGES

Before the Spanish conquerors made their way to Venezuela, the country was inhabited by Indians of culturally diverse tribes, all with their own languages. Historians speculate that the languages spoken then can be divided into four related groups: Cariban, Arawakan, Paezan, and Chibchan. Many tribes and their languages became extinct during the Conquest.

Linguists believe that about 100 distinct languages and dialects are spoken by the Indians living in Venezuela today.

SPANISH NAMES

Many Venezuelans of Spanish heritage have double last names that can be confusing. If a man's name is Pedro Jimenez Garcia, he is called Señor Jimenez. Jimenez is his father's surname and Garcia is his mother's maiden name. The latter distinguishes him from his cousins, who might be Emilio Jimenez Martinez or Jaime Jimenez Rodriquez.

If Pedro Jimenez Garcia marries Maria Estrada Gonzales, she becomes Maria Estrada de Jimenez or Señora de Jimenez. Estrada was her father's name and Gonzales her mother's maiden name, which is now dropped. Their children's surnames will be Jimenez Estrada.

Guajiros speak their own language, but the high degree of assimilation into the mainstream encourages them to also speak Spanish.

STREET NAMES IN CARACAS

In Caracas, an old custom refers to addresses by the names of their corners. In the past, corners were named for the buildings that stood nearby, well-known people who lived there, or events that took place there.

In Plaza Bolívar, for instance, the southeast corner is called *Las Gradillas* or "The Stairs," because at one time, a flight of steps led into the square at that spot. On the south side is a corner called *Las Monjas,* or "The Nuns," a name derived from an 18th-century convent that used to stand there. It was said to have been founded by a rich woman who encouraged the female members of her family to become nuns. At one time there were 70 nuns living in the convent. The building was demolished in 1874.

Five corners in Caracas are named for Our Lady of Mount Carmel, or in Spanish, *La Virgen del Carmen.* The best-known of these is near the Plaza Miranda. It was named *El Carmen* because her image was carved in relief on the facade of a building that once stood there.

One street corner is called *Pelota* after a game that was once played there, and *Hospital* is named for a hospital that stood there. The Marquis of Mijares lived on the corner called *Mijares*, *Diaz* is named for a Dr. Diaz, and so on.

THE NOTION OF SPACE

In Venezuela, as in all cultures, people communicate through body language. Venezuelans, like other Latin Americans, are warm, demonstrative people. They tend to stand very close to one another when conversing. While the typical distance between two North Americans is 21 inches, for Latin Americans it is much less. This may make many North Americans feel uncomfortable, but it is considered unfriendly or cold to back away. Foreigners who work in Venezuela are urged to furnish their offices with a sofa or comfortable chairs placed close together. This is so businessmen and/or women can sit next to each other in a discussion. Talking across a desk can make Venezuelans feel uncomfortable or even snubbed.

Eye contact and a warm manner speak volumes when Venezuelans converse.

Venezuelans tend to touch each other often. When introduced, Venezuelans shake hands. The second time they meet, they are likely to embrace or pat each other on the right shoulder. This custom—the *abrazo* ("ah-BRAH-soh")—is done by both men and women. The shoulder pat is also used to comfort another person or when people are enjoying a good joke. Men and women who are good friends kiss each other to say hello and goodbye, as do women friends. Women often walk arm-in-arm in public.

At a party, it is important to shake hands with each guest upon both arrival and departure, and to look a person in the eye when speaking.

ARTS

VENEZUELANS HAVE a long history of artistic achievements in poetry, music, painting, and oratory. They are also well-known for their Indian pottery, basketry, and weaving.

Caracas is the cultural and artistic center. It is the home of museums and art galleries, including the Museo de Arte Contemporáneo (Museum of Contemporary Art), the Galería de Arte Nacional (National Art Gallery), and the Museo de Bellas Artes (Museum of Fine Arts), which specialize in the works of Venezuelan and internationally renowned artists. The Venezuelan Symphony Orchestra offers concerts ranging from the classical to the modern; it even plays occasionally at subway stations during the rush hour as part of the Metro's cultural program. The city has an accomplished ballet troupe, a national opera company, and several smaller musical ensembles. Architecturally, Caracas has earned a reputation for innovation and imagination, especially through the buildings designed by the country's most famous architect, Carlos Raúl Villanueva.

Above: **At Casa Natal, the birthplace of Simón Bolívar, visitors can see the family bed and Bolívar's library and files.**

Opposite: Gente XX, **a sculpture in various materials, including wood and polychrome. It was executed by Gaudi Este in 1982 and is displayed in the Museo de Bellas Artes, Caracas.**

Colonial homes have been painstakingly restored. The Museo de Arte Colonial, a splendid 18th-century country residence, provides a glimpse of the lifestyle of a wealthy colonial family. The main house, which, in the Spanish tradition, is surrounded by walls, encloses a patio. The rooms are filled with period furniture, paintings, and religious artifacts, and the balconies look out over a garden filled with indigenous orchids. A bathroom in a separate building has a large stone tub into which fresh spring water used to run. Kitchens, storerooms, and stables have been stocked with period utensils, tools, and carriages.

The Catholic influence is apparent in the churches of Venezuela. Above is the Chapel of Santo Domingo.

CULTURAL HISTORY

During the colonial period, it was the Catholic Church that was primarily responsible for encouraging cultural development. Venezuela's scholars and intellectuals were educated in religious schools and their thoughts and writings reflected their religious background. At the same time, the Church was also a great patron of the visual arts: it commissioned paintings and sculptures of religious events and figures for the numerous churches and cathedrals.

In the 18th century, the first portrait paintings began to appear in Venezuela, and in about 1784, the first plays were produced in Caracas' first theater. During the last years of the colonial era, the country was known throughout the Spanish empire for the brilliance of its composers and musicians.

Simón Bolívar was the leading intellectual of the Independence movement. He had extraordinary oratorical abilities and his literary work is still considered to be among the country's finest prose. His tutor, Andrés Bello, a poet and philosopher, wrote the first book to be printed in Venezuela. He left the country with Bolívar in 1810 and eventually settled in Chile where he helped develop the Chilean educational system.

During the Independence period, painting became increasingly important, as subject matter turned toward the political and the historical. Juan Lovera, a self-taught artist, is famous for his group portraits of the leaders of the movement.

Sculpture in bronze, entitled *La Tempestad*, by Lorenzo Gonzalez, in the Museum of Fine Arts.

After Independence, artists rejected the Church's cultural hold and turned for inspiration to the events of the immediate past. Stylistically, however, they kept their European roots. Poets such as José Antonio Martin and Abigaíl Lozano were popular during this time, as was Fermin Toro, who wrote some of Venezuela's first novels.

From 1870 to 1888, during the reign of the dictator Antonio Guzmán Blanco, Venezuela became culturally more sophisticated. A great admirer and patron of the arts, Guzmán Blanco built the Municipal Theater and the first Academy of Fine Arts and appointed French romantic painter, Martín Tovar y Tovar, later known as the "master of Venezuelan mural painting," as his official artist. Tovar y Tovar's follower, Arturo Michelena, became one of South America's best-known painters.

The Maracay bullring built by President Juan Vicente Gómez was designed by Carlos Raúl Villanueva. It was the latter's first design project.

A dictator, Juan Vicente Gómez, who ruled from 1908 to 1935, despised artists and intellectuals, and his reign inspired some of the country's finest political protest writing. Short story writer Rufino Banco Fombona was known for his satiric attacks on the dictator and his followers.

Other early 20th-century writers who helped define the Venezuelan artistic style include Teresa de las Parra, an upper-class woman who wrote an intimate novel about the effect of industrialization (due to the discovery of petroleum) on the life of a *criollo* woman. Romantic poetry written in traditional Spanish couplets was also popular during this period. The leader of the cultural movement, Andrés Eloy Blanco, was known for his lighthearted style and his use of well-known Venezuelan proverbs and myths.

Another of Venezuela's best-known painters, Armando Reverón, emerged during this period. In the spirit of the French impressionists who came before him, Reverón infused his subjects with light and color. He spent much of his life in the small coastal town of Macuto, painting models and landscapes.

RÓMULO GALLEGOS AND *DOÑA BÁRBARA*

Venezuela's most famous novel, published in 1929, is *Doña Bárbara* by Rómulo Gallegos. Translated into many other languages, the novel is considered the finest example of what is known as *criollo* literature, or work that is truly Venezuelan in theme and tone. Like much of Gallegos' work, *Doña Bárbara* is concerned with the theme of the intellectual who struggles to civilize the corrupt and violent elements in Venezuelan society.

The book's hero, Santo Luzardo, represents the civilizing force, and Doña Bárbara, the primary female character, represents the barbaric force. The novel takes place on the *llanos*, which are described as "a wide and stretching land, all horizons like hope, all roads like the will."

Doña Bárbara is a beautiful, imperious woman who is the leader of the *llaneros*. In her youth, her fiancé was killed and she was raped by a group of adventurers. From that point on, she despises men and vows to dominate them. She is skillful with both knife and gun and orders assassination without a thought. At the height of her power, the men of the *llanos*—peons, butlers, landowners, and judges—are all under her control. In the end, Luzardo enlists the help of working-class *llaneros* and overcomes Doña Bárbara and her followers, proving that good will triumph over evil.

Doña Bárbara brought literary fame to Rómulo Gallegos, who later became a well-known politician. He served as director of the ministry of education in Caracas and was a member of both the House of Deputies and the Senate. In 1947, he was elected president, but was ousted after only a few months in office by a military faction. He died in 1969 at the age of 85.

RECENT TRENDS

IN ART With democracy and the economic prosperity that came with the oil boom, public interest in art increased substantially. The government began assigning funds to ambitious artistic projects such as filmmaking, the national symphony, and ballet companies. Artists were exposed to the work of artists from other cultures, especially those of Europe and the United States, and this had a significant impact on their work. At the same time, interest in the native folk art of Venezuela revived.

CREATIVE WRITING In the literary world, historical fiction continues to appeal to many Venezuelans. Authors such as Arturo Uslar Pietri and Miguel Otero Silva have written much admired novels about the Spanish Conquest and 20th-century dictators. In 1980, Luis Britto García achieved great success with *Abrapalabra*, an experimental historical novel that won a coveted literary prize.

Costumed and masked, the performer is, for the moment, one of the audience.

The average Venezuelan young person prefers the novels of Francisco Herrera Luque, which give more colorful, simpler accounts of recent historical events. His *Boves el Urogallo*, about the War of Independence, sold more copies than any novel in Venezuelan history.

THE PERFORMING ARTS The national ballet company, Ballet International de Caracas, was established in 1974 with dancers from all over the world. The company toured Latin America and the United States in the late 1970s. The tone

A music teacher leads a
children's choir in an
open-air rehearsal in
Trujillo.

was Venezuelan: the national dance, the *joropo* ("khoh-ROH-poh"), was
incorporated into a piece, and music by renowned Venezuelan pianist,
Teresa Carreño, was used. Theater continues to be popular in Venezuela.
In 1981, Caracas hosted an international drama festival that brought
together 22 theater groups from 18 countries.

Venezuela's musical groups, including the Maracaibo Symphony
Orchestra, founded in the early 1970s, and the Caracas Opera Company,
have been internationally recognized in recent years. The Venezuelan
Symphony Orchestra is quite popular, as are amateur and professional
opera companies, choruses, and children's musical groups.

PAINTING AND SCULPTURE Venezuelan painters and sculptors have
received attention in the international art world. The work of painter and
sculptor Jesús Raphael Soto, in particular, has been widely exhibited and

Interior of the "Black
Cube" building, Caracas,
designed with steel rods

collected. He has held major exhibitions at the Hirshhorn Gallery in
Washington, D.C., and at the Guggenheim Museum in New York City.
Born in Ciudad Bolívar in 1923, Soto studied in Caracas and Paris. His work
is abstract in nature, influenced by the Dutch painter Piet Mondrian and
the American sculptor Alexander Calder. Many of his pieces move, and he

encourages the viewer to see them from all sides. Soto founded a museum in Ciudad Bolívar that exhibits his own work as well as works of other contemporary artists from North and South America and Europe.

Other well-known Venezuelan painters and sculptors include Alejandro Colina, Francisco Narvaes, and Alejandro Otero. Colina created the famous statue in Caracas of María Lionza atop her tapir, and works by Narvaes and Otero grace many outdoor spaces in Venezuela.

ARCHITECTURE

Primarily through the work of Carlos Raúl Villanueva, Venezuela has become a bastion of architectural achievement. Educated in Paris, Villanueva returned to Caracas to found the College of Architecture at the Central University of Caracas. He supervised the construction of a housing project in one of the poorest neighborhoods of Caracas. Finished in 1943, El Silencio, as the project is known, was the first low-cost housing project to be constructed in Latin America on such a large scale.

Although he went on to design other similar projects, Villanueva's finest work is thought to be the University City in Caracas. Various plazas, canopied walkways, patios, and gardens enhance the structures, as do the murals and sculptures by Alexander Calder, Jean Arp, and Fernand Léger, among others, commissioned by Villanueva himself. Villanueva also designed the Olympic Stadium and the Olympic Pool, the Museum of Fine Arts, and the bullring in Maracay.

Maternity is the name of this sculpture by Lobo, which is sited in front of a building designed by Carlos Raúl Villanueva.

FOLK ARTS

Folk traditions in music, dance, and art have been of particular interest to Venezuelan youths since the early 1960s. Many traditional Venezuelan musical instruments that are played during holidays and religious festivals are Spanish in origin. The *cuatro* ("KWAH-troh"), or four-stringed guitar, which sounds a little like a ukulele, is often played along with the *maracas* ("mah-RAH-cahs"), while people dance the *joropo*, a rhythmic, fast step with many regional variations.

Other dances include the meringue of Caribbean origin, the *tanguito* ("tahn-goo-WEE-toh"), a version of the Argentinean tango, and the waltz. Percussion instruments of African origin are also used in conjunction with

Above and opposite: **In the Orinoco Delta, an Indian weaves a hammock, which may be used by her family or sold at a roadside stall.**

Right: **A roadside craft stall in Mérida selling folk crafts.**

Spanish songs such as *tono* ("TOH-noh") *llanero*, sung by the cowboys.

Native Indians in Venezuela, especially those in the more isolated tribes south of the Orinoco River, have songs (a kind of repetitive chant) for religious events. They also play the flute and a percussion instrument called *culo-en-tierro* ("KOO-loh ehn tih-AIR-roh"), a coconut half that they place on the ground.

Native Indian handicrafts are made for personal use and for sale to tourists. The Guajiro Indians are especially well-known for their ceramics and hammocks, which come in two varieties: the tightly woven *hamaca* and the loosely-woven *chinchorro*. Guajiro women create brightly-colored designs on their large looms at home. They also weave intricately patterned shawls and bags. Guajiro men are famous for their belts and saddlebags. Typical colors are yellow, red, and blue or green.

The Warau Indians of the Orinoco Delta are known for their delicate baskets (woven from dyed palm fibers), hammocks, and stunning carved wooden animals, insects, birds, fish, snakes, and dolphins.

Tribes in the Amazonas Federal Territory—the Makiritare, the Piaroa, and the Yanomami, to name a few—also make beautiful baskets, masks, blowpipes, feather and bead ornaments, rings from black stones, and carved hardwood stools.

The mountain people of the Andes knit sweaters and weave woolen blankets and ponchos called *ruanas* ("roo-AH-nahs"). *Llaneros* are known for their handcrafted leather goods, such as lassos, their rope-soled shoes, and their musical instruments such as the harp, *cuatro*, and *maracas*.

LEISURE

VENEZUELANS SPEND their leisure time either participating in or observing sports activities, or in less formal endeavors such as watching television, listening to the radio, reading the newspaper, or simply chatting among themselves over coffee.

In traditional families, most leisure time is spent with other family members doing family-oriented activities in the home, such as celebrating birthdays or religious holidays. Upper-class families in Caracas spend their free time doing what their North American counterparts do: shopping, watching movies, dining out, or socializing at a private club. In rural parts, the local grocery store is the equivalent of the private club. It is where people—especially men—congregate to relax and discuss the events of the day.

Opposite: **Hiking groups have ample climbing opportunities in Venezuela, as mountain ranges lie in the west, south, and east. This group is hiking on Pico Occidental.**

Left: **Chess in an open space in Caracas is for both spectators and players.**

99

Venezuelans Ozzie Guillén (*far right*) and Carlos Martinez (*right*), who now play for the Chicago White Sox, began their careers with the La Guaira Sharks.

BASEBALL—THE NATIONAL SPORT

Baseball was brought to Venezuela from the United States in the 1890s by a group of upper-class Venezuelan students. In 1895, the first club opened in Caracas. Latin American countries that have the greatest enthusiasm for baseball (Cuba, Nicaragua, the Dominican Republic, Panama, Colombia, and Venezuela) were the nations where the U.S. influence was felt most. Countries where soccer predominates (Brazil, Argentina, Chile, Uruguay, and Peru) had a more powerful European presence.

The earliest Venezuelan teams were made up of the sons of wealthy families living in an affluent suburb of Caracas called El Paraíso, where a baseball field was built in 1902. Soon, street teams of people from all walks of life were formed and the sport gained a broader appeal. After 1918, teams began to be organized more professionally. By 1949, the government instituted a program to build baseball fields and stadiums all over the country.

The professional baseball season in Venezuela lasts from October to February. Some well-known American major leaguers play in Venezuela during their off-season, and vice versa. Venezuelans have played for the

Toronto Blue Jays, the New York Yankees, the Chicago Cubs and White Sox, and the Cincinnati Reds, among others. Recently, Americans from the two Chicago teams and the Atlanta Braves played for the Zulia Eagles, who won the Caribbean Series—the Latin American equivalent of the World Series—in 1989. Other Venezuelan teams include the Caracas Lions, the Magallanes Navigators, the Aragua Tigers, and the Lara Cardinals.

LESSER SPORTS

Soccer, basketball, and boxing are also popular at both the amateur and professional levels. Volleyball games, wrestling matches, and automobile and bicycle races are well attended.

In small towns, people enjoy watching and betting on cockfights. Much money is wagered on these well-trained birds, even though their competitive careers can be over in a matter of minutes.

Betting on racehorses is another favorite activity. The bet, called the *cinco y seis* ("SIN-koh ee SEY-iz," a kind of daily double), has become so popular that the phrase is used to describe any unlikely possibility. The Rinconada Hippodrome in Caracas is one of the most sophisticated tracks in Latin America; it has 2,000 stables and even a swimming pool—for horses. On weekends, 20,000 Venezuelans pack the grandstands to observe the races firsthand; millions of others watch on television.

Traditional Spanish bullfighting is practiced in Venezuela—about 10 bullfights are held each year in Caracas, but most of the matadors come from abroad. Bullfights are also held in Maracay, Valencia, Mérida, and San Cristóbal. Rodeos, or *toros coleados* ("TOH-rohs coh-lay-AH-dors"), are held in small *llanos* towns.

Along the Caribbean coast, water sports such as deep-sea fishing, scuba diving, snorkeling, waterskiing, and sailing are quite popular.

Baseball is to Venezuelans what soccer is to the British—the national obsession. Nearly every town has its own stadium and its own team. Fans cheer with great gusto for their favorite players. Some 200,000 boys, aged 5 to 18, play in amateur leagues.

OTHER AMUSEMENTS

In Caracas and other cities, people often spend their leisure hours at cultural events such as the ballet, the symphony, or the movies. Although Venezuela does have its own filmmaking industry, most of the feature films shown in the commercial theaters are imported from Europe or the United States and dubbed in Spanish. There are more than 650 movie theaters in the country with annual ticket sales of more than 40 million.

Watching television is a common diversion for Venezuelans from all social classes. Television came to the country in 1952. Now, 80% of Venezuelans have regular access to television. There are nearly three million television sets in use and six regular stations, three of them government owned. Having a television set is a status symbol among lower-class people, and it is not uncommon to see television antennas on the roofs of the *ranchos* (shanties) that crowd the outskirts of the urban areas.

Many television shows—*Alf, MASH, Spenser for Hire*, and even the classic *Lassie*—are imported from the United States; others are imported from Latin American countries such as Mexico and Brazil. Programs produced locally are broadcast about half the time. Soap operas, or what are called *telenovelas* ("tay-lay-noh-BAY-lahs"), are extremely popular throughout Latin America. Unlike in the United States, soap operas are shown in Venezuela at night, after the children are asleep. Some of the Venezuelan soaps are so well done that they have been exported to communities in the United States with a high Latin American population.

Radio is also popular in Venezuela. In 1990, there were 150 radio stations and nearly seven million radios in the country. The government also owns eight stations that broadcast mostly cultural and educational programs.

Like their American counterparts, telenovelas *are often about the lives and loves of a host of unsavory characters. In Venezuela, a show called* Pasionaria *("Passionate") was a hit. Telenovelas are also known as* teleculebras *("television snakes") in slang.*

The highest cable car station in the world, at 14,740 feet, is above Mérida in the Venezuelan Andes.

LEISURE AND SOCIAL LIFE

The private club is the center of social activities for the upper classes. On Sundays, the whole family gathers at the club to swim, play tennis, or eat lunch together. Some women even spend weekdays there with friends, either playing cards or having luncheons or tea parties. Men tend to gather there to drink, play dominoes or cards, and have a chat with their male friends.

In rural areas, men gather at the general store on Sundays and in the evenings to drink beer or sugarcane alcohol and, occasionally, play lawn bowling. Women or children who come into the store during these times usually do their business quickly and leave. In very poor areas, social life is even more informal. People tend to chat with their neighbors while they do household chores or are on the patio during a brief moment of inactivity. Full-fledged socializing only takes place during momentous occasions such as weddings and funeral wakes, or during religious festivals.

FESTIVALS

FIESTAS OR FESTIVALS in Venezuela are usually religious, although some have political origins. All of Venezuela celebrates Christmas, Easter, and Independence Day, but some of the other holidays, such as patron saints' days, are celebrated only in certain towns or villages. The same patron saints' days can be observed differently from one village to the next, although most include fireworks, processions, street dances, and games. Depending on the history of the town, festival customs can have an African, Spanish, or Indian flavor, or a mixture of all three.

Holidays are a form of family recreation in Venezuela. In the larger cities, some holidays, such as Holy Week (the week before Easter), have lost their religious significance and have become times for family vacations. Many urbanites—and nearly all *caraqueños*—leave the city during Holy Week to travel abroad or to visit relatives in nearby states. In many Andean towns, however, Holy Week is celebrated with great vigor: passion plays are acted out, robed and hooded repentants go to Mass on their knees, and large images of Judas are burned in the town square.

Above: **The celebration of Dia de San Pedro**

Opposite: **Everybody loves to watch a band on parade, a regular feature of major festivals in Venezuela.**

In many rural areas, religious festivals and patron saints' days provide the only real entertainment for farming families during the year. Festivities sponsored by local religious groups, merchants, or prominent citizens give people a chance to meet old friends, see family members, watch cockfights, attend special Masses and elaborate processions, and dance, drink, and listen to music all night.

OFFICIAL HOLIDAYS IN VENEZUELA

Jan 1	New Year's Day
Feb/Mar	Two days of Carnival
	Ash Wednesday
Mar/Apr	Holy Thursday, Good Friday, Easter
Apr 19	Declaration of Independence
May 1	Labor Day (often also Ascension and Corpus Christi Day)
June 24	Battle of Carabobo
July 5	Independence Day
July 24	Simón Bolívar's Birthday
Oct 12	Columbus Day
Nov 1	All Saints' Day
Dec 17	Death of Simón Bolívar
Dec 24	Christmas Eve
Dec 25	Christmas Day
Dec 31	New Year's Eve

CARNIVAL

In Caracas and some other towns, the principal fiesta is Carnival, a two-day celebration that takes place in either February or March on the Monday or Tuesday before Ash Wednesday. Carnival is the last festivity before the six-week-long sobering period of Lent takes over. Hence, people dress up in wild costumes, dance in the streets, and live a bit recklessly with full knowledge that a time of personal sacrifice and religious contemplation will follow. Most stores and businesses are closed during Carnival.

The festivities begin with a large parade complete with decorated floats and people dressed in colorful costumes. Some entire streets are roped off during the whole festival so people can dance the *joropo* and other Venezuelan dances and sing traditional songs. In Caracas, water fights are common during Carnival, and people are known to decorate statues of Simón Bolívar with wreaths and flowers. In the town of El Callao in Bolívar State, calypso music of Caribbean origin is played, while in the German village of Colonia Tovar, a mock funeral is held to mark the end of the festivities.

Opposite: **The Devil Dancers of Yare during Corpus Christi**

CORPUS CHRISTI

This is probably the most colorful festival in Venezuela. Celebrated on the Thursday after Trinity Sunday, it takes place about nine weeks after Easter in the town of San Francisco de Yare in Miranda State (near Caracas) and in some villages in the states of Aragua and Carabobo.

Legend has it that a humble nun, Saint Juliana, often had visions while praying. One day, Christ appeared and indicated to her the meaning of her visions: the lack of a festival in honor of the Blessed Sacrament. Thus, the Festival of Corpus Christi honors the Eucharist (the consecrated bread and wine consumed during a Catholic Mass to symbolize the body and blood of Christ).

For the famous festival that takes place in San Francisco de Yare, people dress up in baggy red costumes with crosses pinned to them, carry rosaries, and wear papier-mâché horned masks that resemble frightening bulls' heads. They are called the Devil Dancers.

At 6:00 a.m. on the morning of the festival, the dancers gather in front of the village church and dance vigorously to the beat of Venezuelan music. They attend Mass in the church and then return to their dancing, which by now has become even fiercer. After this they visit the homes of important people in the village, who give them money or liquor.

In the afternoon, another procession symbolizing the Eucharist forms near the church; each time it approaches the Devil Dancers, the members of the procession recoil in fear. Finally, all return to the church, where the Devils take off their masks and receive the communion.

It is believed that the dancing and musical styles used during the celebration of Corpus Christi in San Francisco de Yare derive directly from non-Christian rituals practiced by the Ayoman Indians who used to inhabit that region.

CHRISTMAS IN VENEZUELA

The celebration of Christmas in Venezuela has undergone rather drastic changes in recent years. In the old days, people used to set up a *nacimiento* ("nah-sih-mih-EHN-toh"), or nativity scene, in the patio or living room of their homes. It contained small carved images of the holy family, the wise men, the shepherds and their sheep, the ox, the donkey, and a star. The background contained lifelike houses, lakes, roads, and people, and the whole scene was placed on folded cloth that resembled mountains. Living-room windows would be left open so passersby could admire the *nacimiento,* and the family would gather there in the evening to sing carols or to recount the Christmas story. The figure of Jesus as a baby was placed in the manger only on Christmas Eve, and the figures of the Three Kings were situated far from the child and moved up a little bit every day until they reached him on January 6, or Epiphany.

Venezuelan children did not know Santa Claus. They actually received their gifts from the Three Kings on Epiphany, instead of on Christmas Day. They placed their shoes under their beds on the night of January 5, and in the morning the shoes were filled with such things as small toys, fruit, or other foods.

Christmas in Venezuela

It was also traditional to begin attending Christmas Mass as early as December 16, at 4:00 a.m.! After Mass, churchgoers would be met by people singing carols and playing *maracas;* then they would probably drink the traditional after-Mass cup of sweetened black coffee and munch on a crispy corn fritter called a *masa* ("MAH-sah"), which might be purchased from a woman frying them on a small grill near the curb

More recently, Christmas celebrants, especially young people, would rollerskate in the village plaza all night long, indulge in hot chocolate and long fried doughnuts in the shape of twisted ropes, and then attend Mass at dawn.

Although the various traditions still take place in some areas, they have been steadily dying out. The typical Venezuelan Christmas today resembles the typical North American Christmas. Gifts from Santa Claus rather than the Three Kings are wrapped in festive paper and placed under the Christmas tree to be opened on Christmas morning.

One Venezuelan Christmas tradition that has not been lost, however, is the inclusion of music in the celebration. Young people train for months to compete in Christmas music competitions in which *gaitas* ("GAY-tahs"), or bands playing traditional Venezuelan instruments, attempt to outperform each other. A *gaita* is usually made up of a four-stringed guitar, or *cuatro*, a common drum, *maracas*, and an unusual percussion instrument called a *furruco* ("foo-ROO-koh"). This is a drum with a hole in the center into which a long stick is placed and rubbed up and down to create a strange, hoarse, resonant sound.

Gaitas go from house to house at Christmas, especially in Caracas, playing traditional music and accompanied by choruses singing Venezuelan songs.

Opposite and below: **While the Venezuelan** *naci-miento* **is being replaced by the North American Christmas tree, the traditional** *furruco* **is still very much a part of Christmas celebrations.**

PATRON SAINTS' DAYS

Nearly every Venezuelan village has a patron saint, and a festival held in his or her honor takes place annually. It is customary to carry images of the patron saint through the streets in formal procession, after which dances, bullfights, competitions (such as climbing a greased pole), rodeos, and even beauty contests are held.

East of Caracas, in the village of Guatire, celebrants honor St. Peter by blackening their faces and donning top hats. St. Peter used to be invoked throughout the Christian world against fever because, according to the Bible, Christ cured St. Peter's mother-in-law of a fever. Village legend in Guatire has it that a slave woman's child was cured through her prayers to St. Peter. She danced all day to offer her thanks to the saint. St. Peter's Day, therefore, is celebrated with wild dancing that is said to resemble that of the Devil Dancers on Corpus Christi.

The festival of St. John is celebrated primarily on the Caribbean coast in Miranda State, which has a large black population. This festival has elements that are distinctly African in origin. The framework of the fiesta is Spanish, but the music that accompanies the dancing is played on drums common to Africa. The festival is associated with the summer festivals of pre-Christian times where fires were lit to greet the beginning of summer and celebrants gathered round and jumped through the fires and sang traditional songs praising both the saint and summer. Taking place from June 23 through June 25, the festival of St. John is remarkable for its unrelenting street dancing.

The festival of St. Benito (St. Benedict) on December 27 also has a strong African heritage, although it is now celebrated by Venezuelans of all ethnic groups. In the area near Lake Maracaibo, St. Benito is honored differently from village to village. The Paruajano Indians of Sinamaica

Lagoon place images of the saint in boats and sail to a designated area where a special altar has been erected to honor him. Then, the drumming starts and the villagers take turns dancing with images of the saint. In El Mojan, which is very close to the lagoon, *criollo* celebrants carry saint figures through the streets, dancing an entirely different step to the music of the *cuatro* and different drums. In Gibraltar and Bobures, black people celebrate with yet another form of dancing that is distinctly African in tempo. In Timotes, in Mérida state, dancers carry *maracas*, blacken their faces with paint, and wear black grass skirts and headdresses with feathers. Others don the traditional Venezuelan *liquiliqui* or wear a cowboy-like costume with a red fringe.

The celebration of Dia de San Benito in Santo Domingo

FOOD

THE CUISINE OF VENEZUELA—like its religious rituals, customs, and language—shows Indian, Spanish, and African influences. Many staples of the Venezuelan diet were cultivated by the Indians in precolonial days, and many of the ingredients commonly used today in Venezuelan dishes originally came from Spain or Africa during the colonial period.

The early Indians of South America cultivated corn, beans, and squash. Upon their arrival in the New World, the Spanish conquistadors found other foods such as avocados, Brazil nuts, chocolate, guavas, manioc (bitter cassava), papayas, passion fruit, pineapples, and tomatoes. Many of these foods traveled back to Spain with the conquerors, who, in turn, brought chickens, pigs, garlic, onions, olive oil, rice, *garbanzo* ("bar-BAHN-zoh") beans (chickpeas), and sugarcane to South America.

Coffee—the most beloved drink of South America—originated in Ethiopia and made its way to South America via the Middle East. Bananas and plantains, which are very much a part of the Venezuelan diet, came to the New World from Africa and the Canary Islands, although they originated in India and Malaysia.

Many of the ingredients brought from the outside world were readily accepted into the Venezuelan diet. Over the years, they were changed and adapted to suit the *criollo* palate, and what emerged was a Venezuelan cuisine that in many ways is unique, although some cooking traditions are shared with other Latin American cultures.

VENEZUELAN SPECIALTIES

THE *AREPA* The *arepa* ("ah-RAY-pah"), which is of Indian origin, is a staple of the Venezuelan diet. The standard variety, which resembles a very thick Mexican tortilla, is made by mixing either yellow or white corn flour with salt and enough water to make a dough. After being formed

Opposite: **Market vendors display their goods in the open space of a Venezuelan marketplace.**

115

Arepas on a griddle, ready to be sold at this roadside stall

into balls or patties, the *arepa* is toasted on a griddle, wrapped in a napkin, and served in a straw basket. To enhance their flavor, *arepas* are often stuffed with ground beef, cheese, avocado, tuna, ham, eggs, beans, shrimp, and even shark. The basic *arepa* is almost tasteless. The stuffed varieties, however, are delicious.

Caraqueños often eat *arepas* in restaurants called *areperas* ("ah-ray-PAIR-rahs") rather than at home, although prepared *arepa* flour is available in grocery stores.

BLACK BEANS Black beans are another favorite Venezuelan dish that crosses all economic boundaries. One of the simplest and most delicious recipes using black beans is affectionately called *Caviar Criollo,* or "Native Caviar," by Venezuelans.

The national dish of Venezuela is also made with black beans. The main ingredients in *Pabellon* ("pah-bell-lih-OHN") *Criollo*—black beans, rice, and steak—are cooked separately and served on a platter topped with sautéed bananas. This dish is based on a 16th-century Spanish recipe called *Ropa Vieja* ("ROH-pah bih-EH-hah"), or "Old Clothes." Many Venezuelans agree that this dish cannot possibly be made well in a restaurant but must be prepared at home, according to secret family recipes.

Aside from the home favorites, Caracas and major cities in Venezuela have a wide variety of ethnic restaurants that serve Arab, Chinese, Japanese, Hungarian, Portuguese, Colombian, Mexican, Trinidadian, Cuban, Swiss, or German food.

CAVIAR CRIOLLO
(serves 6)

Ingredients:
1 cup dried black beans
1 large onion, coarsely chopped
5 tablespoons olive oil
1 red chili, seeded and crushed
3 cloves garlic, crushed
2 teaspoons ground cumin
salt

Preparation:
1. Cook the black beans for about an hour in lightly salted water until they are tender. Drain.

2. Sauté the onion in just 2 tablespoons of olive oil until soft. Add the chili, garlic, and ground cumin, and cook for 2 minutes. Add the beans, the remaining olive oil, and salt to taste. Mix and serve as a side dish with chicken or grilled beef.

THE *HALLACA* A dish that unifies the national cuisine is the *hallaca* ("hah-lih-AH-kah"). Traditionally made at Christmas, the *hallaca* is the dish that Venezuelans yearn for when they are away from home. They say only a woman can cook the *hallaca* properly, after years of practice and with the help of the whole family. Invented by the Indians in precolonial days, *hallacas* are essentially little pies of corn dough that are filled with meat, chicken, or other ingredients, wrapped inside a banana leaf in a flat rectangle, and boiled. The banana leaf seals in and enhances the flavor of the *hallaca*.

Cooking a traditional meal in a modern kitchen in Caracas.

Different regions add their own special touches: eggs, olives, raisins, or vegetables. But, no matter what the ingredients, a platter of *hallacas* occupies the place of honor on the Christmas Eve table.

DESSERTS

Several Venezuelan dishes are made using coconut or coconut milk: rice dishes, meat stews and soups, and especially desserts. A famous Venezuelan cake, *Bien Me Sabe de Coco* ("bih-ehn may SAH-bay day KOH-koh"), is made by moistening plain cake with muscatel wine and coconut cream. Coconut is also used in candies or combined with caramel to make what is called a *coquito* ("koh-KIH-toh").

Flan, a type of Spanish pudding of baked egg custard with a caramel topping, is also served for dessert as are a wide variety of tropical fruits such as mango, guava, pineapple, and papaya.

COFFEE: MOST IMPORTANT BEVERAGE

South Americans are great coffee drinkers. They drink a cup at each meal and several times in between meals. Friends often meet each other in the street and go to a café or a little outdoor coffee stand to indulge in a cup of coffee and some satisfying gossip.

Although about half the world's coffee is now grown in Latin America, the plant itself originally came from Africa. From there, it traveled to the Arab nations where it became an acceptable stimulant for Muslims, who are forbidden to drink alcohol. Coffee arrived in Europe with the Turkish invaders in the early 1600s, and in Latin America in the 1720s. Brazil and Colombia are famous for their excellent coffee, and the Venezuelan crop, though small, is said to be good. In fact, Venezuela produces the famous *café azul de Caracas* ("KAH-fay ah-ZOOL day kah-RAH-kass"), or the blue coffee bean of Caracas, which is of the highest quality.

Coffee drinking is so popular in Venezuela that different varieties have a vocabulary all their own: *café-con-leche* ("KAH-fay-kon-LAY-chay") is coffee with hot milk; a large cup of mild black coffee is called a *guayoyo* ("goo-ay-YOH-yoh"); a *negro* ("NAY-groh") is a large cup of strong black coffee; a *negrito* ("nay-GRIH-toh") is a small cup or demitasse of strong black coffee; a *cafecito* ("kah-fay-SIH-toh") is a demitasse of sweetened coffee; a large cup of strong coffee with a little milk added is called a *marron* ("mah-ROHN"); and a demitasse of the same brew is called a *marroncito* ("mah-rahn-SIH-toh").

Coffee knows no class barriers in South America; it is enjoyed by both subsistence farmer and wealthy entrepreneur.

119

EATING OUT IN CARACAS AND BEYOND

Caraqueños eat out regularly and often. Whether they opt for a pizza parlor, McDonald's, or a famous French restaurant in an elegant hotel, *caraqueños* have a great variety to choose from. The most popular places to eat include *criollo* restaurants, which specialize in local cuisine, pasta places, *areperas* (which are often open all night), steak houses specializing in Argentinean cuisine, and Spanish restaurants where *tascas* ("TAHS-cahs"), or grilled seafood snacks, are offered and dining is accompanied by Spanish music.

A soft drinks stall in Maracaibo. Many people find work selling food and drink on the streets.

Restaurateurs use ingredients that are grown only in Venezuela for some recipes: rice from Guárico state, tomatoes and miniature peppers from Margarita Island, freshwater prawns and lobsters from the Caribbean, beef from the *llanos*. After dinner, many young people like to spend time in piano bars or cafés, enjoying coffee, fresh fruit shakes, and dessert.

Caracas has the most sophisticated international cuisine, but many states have famous dishes of their own: Zulia is known for fish from Lake Maracaibo and plantains; Trujillo is known for pastries and braised chicken; Mérida for dishes made from local chickpeas and green peas; Falcón for goat's meat recipes and cheese and fudge made from goat's milk; Bolívar for fish stews; the Caribbean states for an array of fresh seafood dishes including *pargo* ("PAR-goh"), or red snapper; and Táchira for chicken soup made with milk and hot peppers.

EATING AT HOME

The typical Caracas family breakfasts at 6:00 a.m. or 6:30 a.m. so the children can be in school by 7:00 a.m. Standard breakfast fare includes eggs, *arepas*, bread or rolls, fresh fruit juice, and coffee. Lunch is served from noon to 2:00 p.m. and is the most important meal of the day. A typical lunch consists of soup, salad, meat and vegetables, fruit, and dessert, which is often a pastry or tart. Water, soft drinks, beer, or lemonade is drunk with lunch. Dinner is usually a light meal, which is served at about 9:00 p.m. *Arepas*, soup, and a sandwich or eggs are typical dinner fare. Some people have hot chocolate before bed or at breakfast; men drink whiskey, beer, rum, or wine at the cocktail hour. Venezuelan women rarely drink beer or alcoholic spirits.

Attractive colors and sweets attract these children to a vendor at a fair.

Although lunch is the most significant meal of the day for families in Venezuela, dinner is the meal most associated with entertaining. Some dinner parties begin as late as 11:00 p.m., and do not end until 3:00 a.m. or later. Even if a dinner begins early, it can end as late as midnight. The wife and husband usually sit at the head and foot of the table, with the guest of honor next to one or the other.

At upper-class gatherings, the food will be served by a maid, and guests are not permitted to start eating until everybody at the table has been served. Venezuelans do not push their guests to finish everything on their plates or to have additional helpings. Once diners have finished, they often place the knife and fork together, with the tips pointing in the direction of 10:00 o'clock.

CARIBBEAN SEA

A   B   C   D

N

1

Punto Fijo
Coro
Margarita Is.
La Asunción
TRINIDAD AND TOBAGO
San Rafael
Maracaibo
CARACAS
Carúpano
Port of Spain
Cabimas
Barcelona
Cumaná
Ciudad Ojeda
Barquisimeto
Valencia
Maracay
Maracaibo Lake
Anaco

2

Trujillo
San Carlos
Valle de la Pascua
Tucupita
Valera
Guanare
El Tigre
Curiapo
Mérida
Barinas
Ciudad Guayana
Pico Bolívar (16,427 ft.)
Ciudad Bolívar
San Cristóbal
Apure
Orinoco
El Dorado
Elorza
Puerto Páez
Paragua
Poci
Angel Falls (3,212 ft.)
GUYA

3

COLOMBIA
Puerto Ayacucho
Caroní
Mt. Roraima (2,810 ft.)
San Fernando de Atabapo
Orinoco
Casiquiare

● Capital city
● Major town
▲ Mountain peak

Height of land (feet)
over 9,000
6,000 – 9,000
3,000 – 6,000
1,500 – 3,000
600 – 1,500
0 – 600

4

VENEZUELA

BRAZIL

122

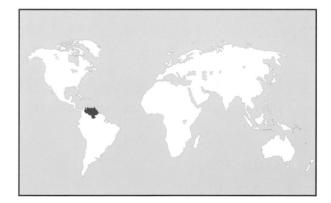

QUICK NOTES

LAND AREA
352,143 square miles

POPULATION
20.6 million

CAPITAL
Caracas

NATIONAL ANTHEM
Glorio al Bravo Pueblo que el Yugo Lanzo
("Glory to the Brave Nation that Shook off
the Yoke")

FLAG
Three horizontal bands—yellow, blue, and
red—with an arc of seven white stars in the
blue portion

NATIONAL TREE
Aranguery

STATES AND TERRITORIES
Anzoátegui, Apure, Aragua, Barinas, Bolívar,
Carabobo, Cojedes, Falcón, Guárico, Lara,
Mérida, Miranda, Monagas, Nueva Esparta,
Portuguesa, Sucre, Táchira, Trujillo,
Yaracuy, Zulia; Amazonas (territory), Delta
Amacuro (territory), Federal District of
Caracas

MAJOR RIVERS
Orinoco, Apure, and Caroni

MAJOR LAKES
Maracaibo and Valencia

HIGHEST POINT
Pico Bolívar (16,427 feet)

HIGHEST FALLS
Angel Falls (3,212 feet)

OFFICIAL LANGUAGE
Spanish

MAJOR RELIGION
Roman Catholicism

CURRENCY
Bolívar ($1 = 14.50 bolívars)

MAIN EXPORTS
Petroleum, iron ore, coffee, steel, aluminum,
cocoa

IMPORTANT ANNIVERSARY
Declaration of Independence (Apr 19)

LEADERS IN POLITICS
Simón Bolívar (1783–1830)—revolutionary
leader in the fight for independence;
Venezuela's most beloved hero
Rómulo Betancourt (1908–81)—leader of
Acción Democrática; president 1945–48
and 1959–64

GLOSSARY

abrazo   ("ah-BRAH-soh") An embrace between Venezuelans when they meet.

caraqueño   ("kah-rah-KAIR-nyoh") Inhabitant of Caracas.

comadre   ("kom-MAH-dray") Godmother.

compadre   ("kom-PAH-dray") Godfather.

criollo   ("kree-OH-loh") Creole. Originally a person of Spanish ancestry born in the New World; now describes someone or something that is truly Venezuelan or indigenous to Venezuela.

cuatro   ("KWAH-troh") Small guitar with four strings.

hacienda   ("ah-sih-EHN-dah") Large plantation or estate.

hamaca   ("ah MAH kah") A tightly-woven hammock.

llanero   ("yah-NAIR-roh") One who dwells in the *llanos*, usually the cowboy.

llanos   ("YAH-noss") Vast central plains of Venezuela.

manta   ("MAHN-tah") Intricately woven shawl worn by Spanish and Latin American women.

mestizo   ("mehs-TEE-soh") Originally a person of mixed Spanish-Indian ancestry; now refers to anyone of mixed racial descent.

piñata   ("pih-NYAH-tah") Brightly-colored animal figure filled with candy and toys and broken apart at children's birthday parties.

quinceañera   ("kin-seh-ah-nih-AIR-rah") A girl's 15th birthday.

rancho   ("RAHN-choh") Makeshift home constructed on the outskirts of large Venezuelan cities, especially Caracas.

tepui   ("tair-POO-ee") Flat-topped rock formation in the Guiana Highlands.

Venezolano   ("beh-neh-zoh-LAH-noh") Venezuelan.

BIBLIOGRAPHY

Blutstein, Howard I.: *Area Handbook for Venezuela*, U.S. Government Printing Office, Washington, D.C., 1977.

Country Report: Venezuela, 4th Quarter 1993, The Economist Intelligence Unit, London, 1993.

Devine, Elizabeth and Nancy L. Braganti: *The Traveler's Guide to Latin American Customs and Manners*, St. Martin's Press, New York, NY, 1988.

Ewell, Judith: *Venezuela, A Century of Change*, Stanford University Press, Stanford, CA, 1984.

Fodor's South America, Fodor's Travel Publications, Inc., New York and London, 1989.

Lanier, Alison R.: *Venezuela*, Intercultural Press, Chicago, IL, 1981.

South America, Central America & The Caribbean 1993, Europa Publications Ltd, London, 1992.

Venezuela in Pictures, Lerner Publications Company, Minneapolis, MN, 1987.

INDEX

INDEX

INDEX

PICTURE CREDITS